Teaching on

BORROWED
TIME

An Adjunct's Memoir

LAURENCE C. SCHWARTZ

PAGE PUBLISHING
Conneaut Lake, PA

First originally published by Page Publishing 2021

ISBN 978-1-6624-5654-1 (pbk)
ISBN 978-1-6624-5655-8 (digital)

Printed in the United States of America

Dedicated to my mother, Sheila.

Adjunct: a person associated with lesser status, rank, authority, etc., in some duty or service; assistant. a person working at an institution, as a college or university, without having full or permanent status: My lawyer works two nights a week as an adjunct, teaching business law at the college.

—Dictionary.com

I've read anthropological papers written about people like me. We're called marginal, as if we exist anywhere but on the center of the page. We are parked in the bleachers looking into the arena, never the main players, but there are bonuses to peripheral vision. Out beyond the normal bounds, you at least know where you're not. You escape the claustrophobia of belonging, and what you lack in security you gain by realizing—as those insiders never do—that security is an illusion... "Caught between two worlds," is the way we're often characterized, but I'd put it differently. We are the catch.

—Louise Erdrich and Michael
Dorris's *The Crown of Columbus*

O, che dolce cosa e questa prospettiva!
—Giorgio Vasari on the work
of Paolo Voccello

In chaos, there is fertility.
—Anais Nin

ACKNOWLEDGMENTS

I wish to thank the few men and women who encouraged me early in my adjunct career and who lent an ear to the new kid on the block. I would also like to thank my family for their support.

Some of the names of the characters have been changed.

PART I

OTHELLO THE MOOR

While walking south on Lexington Avenue on a gray fall morning, I thought of a scene from the film *Escape from Alcatraz*. The warden, played by that splendid actor Patrick McGoohan, confronted a recently arrived convict, played by Clint Eastwood. It was obvious through the warden's clipped speech patterns and stiff upper lip that he felt that his authority was being threatened. The warden had been informed that Eastwood's convict had a knack of outsmarting his incarcerators. The warden was worried at the prospect that the convict might attempt and ultimately succeed at escaping from the Rock.

I have never seen *Escape from Alcatraz* in its entirety, which is strange because prison drama is one of my favorite film genres. I know that Eastwood's convict did indeed escape, but it remained a mystery if he survived the rocky waters of San Francisco Bay. Inversely, I've *survived* but have given up any hope of escaping. I am a lifer.

That gray fall morning occurred in September 1989. I was walking to the number 6 train on Sixty-Eighth Street. I rode to Forty-Second Street and changed trains to a number 4. From there, I rode into Brooklyn and got off at Nevins Street. Ascending the stairs leading to Dekalb Avenue, I found myself facing the downtown Brooklyn campus of Long Island University—and my very first day teaching at a college.

My teaching title would be that of adjunct lecturer. I have been an Adjunct Lecturer ever since. I have taught at twenty different colleges: Long Island University (downtown Brooklyn Campus),

Kingsborough Community College—CUNY, Brooklyn College—CUNY, Queens College—CUNY, Queensborough Community College—CUNY, New York City College of Technology—CUNY, La Guardia Community College—CUNY, Bronx Community College—CUNY, Yeshiva University, St. Joseph's College, Mercy College, Hofstra University, College of New Rochelle (Rosa Parks Campus), College of New Rochelle (Brooklyn Campus), Borough of Manhattan Community College—CUNY, Medgar Evers College—CUNY, SUNY Empire State College, Tobit College, Laboratory Institute of Merchandising, Bergen Community College.

I have taught twenty-three different subjects: Oral Communications, Interpersonal Communications, Intercultural Communications, Mass Media in America, Art History, The Language of Film, Introduction to Cinema, Understanding Movies, Introduction to the Thriller, Introduction to Theatre, Introduction to Opera, the Golden Age of Radio, Voice and Diction, Introduction to Acting, Expository Composition, English Modes, the History of American Music, Public Speaking, Business Communication, Introduction to the Arts, Mass Communications and Society, Remedial English, The Hollywood Western.

I taught The Hollywood Western at Mercy College, at its Dobbs Ferry campus. Six days before the beginning of the semester, I got a phone call from Paul Trent, coordinator of media studies.

"How'd ya like to teach another film course?" Paul asked.

The Hollywood Western had never been offered before. I had to develop a syllabus as well as choose a textbook. It was a good thing I was a cinephile, for I embraced the experience. It was a lark of sorts in self-education. This had happened to me quite frequently in the past few years. For example, in the fall semester of 2014, ten days before the semester began, I was assigned my courses at Tobit College: Mass Media in America and Introduction to the Visual Arts. I had no problem with the former because I'd taught Mass Media in America thrice before at three different colleges; however, Introduction to the Visual Arts presented a grand challenge.

The course should have been called Art History. It surveyed ancient civilizations, medieval painting, the Renaissance, classical and modern architecture, sculpture, some modern masters (like Van Gogh, Cezanne, Picasso), and alternative forms of art into the twenty-first century. As Cassius related to Brutus when he alluded to Caesar's challenge to swim the waters of the Tiber, I "plunged in" to the study of art history, and when I "bade" my students "to follow," they did. There was a shared enthusiasm. I had a hell of a lot of fun describing moonlit oceans, the play of sunlight and shade upon leaves, color schemes, Van Gogh's troubled life, and George Grosz's eerily playful depiction of debauchery. There were worse ways to earn one's keep.

Now when I hear the word *saint*, my mind summons the dual interpretations Caravaggio brought to his conception of Saint Matthew. Now I can sit in a personal bank advisor's office and appreciate the framed copy of an abstract work hanging on the wall. Now I can even think of myself as having been Modigliani in a former life because, as a lifelong advanced doodler, I've discovered the distinct similarity Modigliani and I have of elongating the face, neck, and nose. I never knew this similarity existed before I started teaching him. In addition, we both have trouble holding our certain appetites in check.

I didn't plan on becoming an adjunct. I planned on becoming an actor. And I did. At age twenty-three, not more than two years after earning my BFA in acting from Boston University's School of Fine Arts, I landed a role in an original gay farce, *Max's Millions*. Auditions were held at the No Smoking Playhouse on West Forty-Fifth Street in the heart of the Theater District. It was an open call. They were looking for good-looking actors in their twenties. The line of actors waiting to be seen began on the sidewalk in front of the theater and extended a good two hundred feet east toward Eight Avenue. The purpose of the open call was to simply type out actors through their appearance. I walked on stage with a few other actors and just stood there, as if waiting to be auctioned. We were asked to turn around and then asked to face front again.

A few days later, I received a phone call from the production stage manager. She asked me to come in and read for the part of Bonano Bon Giovani, an Olympic wrestler from New Jersey. The initial run was a sixteen-performance Actors' Equity—approved showcase. At the completion of the run, one of the associate producers invested fifty thousand dollars that would advance the production to an off-off-Broadway mini contract, which was the lowest tier of professional status. I received my Actors' Equity card and a favorable review in *The New York Times*. The play itself received a middling review and closed after ten performances. Now I had professional union status and the opportunity to attend Equity Principal Auditions. It was a union requirement for all Equity-contracted shows to hold Equity Principal Auditions. Broadway plays and Off-Broadway plays were seldom cast through Equity Principal Auditions. They were cast through agent submissions. I didn't have an agent. Broadway and Off-Broadway musicals would cast the chorus and dancers through open calls, but I wasn't a musical performer. When I attended an Equity Principal Audition, I was truly one of a herd.

Like many young actors in New York City, I earned my living by waiting tables. Sign-ups for auditions started an hour before they began. In order to ensure an audition slot, actors would arrive at the audition site *at least* an hour before sign-up. If an audition began at nine, an actor could arrive at seven and wait the hour when the sign-up began. Sometimes actors would arrive *two* hours before sign-up began. For summer stock productions, it was common to see at least one hundred actors lined up on the sidewalk at the audition site at five in the morning. You'd wait the morning out until sign-up and be one of the first to audition. Or you could wait the morning out and be given a stub. This meant that you could leave the audition site and return later in the day to audition. This was the method I used when I worked the lunch shift.

Many EPAs were held at Actors' Equity Association at 146 West Forty-Sixth Street. I would wait among the herd in the wee hours. Some actors brought portable folding chairs. At first, it wasn't so much the waiting in line that bothered me as it was that very seldom did any words come from actors' mouths that weren't related to either acting or the theatre. The conversations I heard were usually about auditions or callbacks or "I'm going to get new headshots next week" or "I did some extra work last week in an independent film," or "Yeah, I was up to Writers and Artists Agency last month, and they seemed interested."

I'd wake in the wee hours of the morning, arrive at the audition site, sign up for a time slot, and receive a stub allowing me to return later in the day for my actual two-minute audition. After working my lunch shift, I returned to the audition site, waited until my name called, took a place on a short line, and finally, got a chance to do a two-minute monologue. Even though contracted Equity productions in New York City seldom, if ever, cast through open calls, it wasn't a total waste of time for actors to attend. You were being seen by people in the industry. If you were good, your headshot might end up in an "active file." It gave the actor the chance to perfect the audition monologue or try out new monologues.

I knew what I was doing wasn't easy, but the more auditions I attended, the more I thought they were a waste of *my* time. But I persevered. Landing a role in *Max's Millions* from an open call and receiving a favorable review in *The New York Times* were clear indications of workmanlike ability.

Some months after *Max's Millions* closed, someone recommended a weekly private class taught by Suzanne Shepherd. In order to join Suzanne's class, you had to do a monologue for her. I chose one from a little-known play, *In the Clap Shack* by William Styron. The play is set in 1943 on the Urological Ward of the United States Naval Hospital on a Marine Corps base in the South. The character I chose—Schwartz—is speaking at the death bed of a fellow soldier who is Black. Through the quotations of a world-renowned rabbi and his own emotional appeals, Schwartz is trying to rid Lorenzo of his racism.

After I completed the monologue, Suzanne began thinking, carefully considering her words. I was already impressed.

"You know something?" she began. "I get the feeling that you're trying to be very effective."

"Why do you say that?"

"You're showing us how good an actor you are. You're almost telecasting that you're a serious actor and committed to acting the part. Acting? That man you're playing doesn't know he's acting. He's sitting at the deathbed of a man and trying to convert him to love from hatred before the man dies. You're probably the last person in the world that Lorenzo is going to see. Maybe you might give *that* some thought instead of trying to show us how good an actor you are."

She had me, and she knew me for all of five minutes. Suzanne offered fresh, constructive criticism in a firm but humane manner. Under Suzanne, I grew as an actor and as a person. She made me understand that, to be a good teacher, you needed to have a feel for people as well as expertise of subject. It's not always necessary to be liked in order to be an effective teacher, and I was certain that it was a low priority for law professors and not even given a second thought by professors at medical schools. But when it came to teaching the arts as applied skills or teaching undergraduate courses in the humanities to students who had taken them as electives, a teacher who exuded warmth and elan would probably be listened to.

Suzanne summed it up when she said to me one day, "You're a much better actor than how you turned out from Boston University."

By studying with Suzanne, I started to understand what it meant to be a genuinely good actor. I continued making the rounds of auditions and waiting tables to support myself.

In the spring of '86, I was recommended for a small role in a non-Equity showcase of Brendan Behan's *The Quare Fellow*. I had worked with Evan Kitrell, the lead, some two and a half years earlier in a production of Lewis John Carlino's one-act play *Objective Case*. When the role of Prisoner E became available after the actor dropped out, Evan called me and suggested that I come to a rehearsal and meet Stuart, the director. Stuart offered me the part on the spot. *The Quare Fellow* is set in a prison, and the tension rests upon the imminent hanging of one of the inmates. It is a very Irish play exploring both social and political issues nascent to the land of Eire. It has a healthy peppering of Irish idioms and the occasional bubbling of Gaelic.

There were times when the actors were at sea. Characterizations organically grew, but we were all American actors with little to no professional experience. A strong directorial hand was needed.

Luckily for me, I didn't need a director's help because my part was so small, and my character's intentions were very straightforward. I only appeared briefly in one scene. It took place in the prison yard. The inmates were arguing about the exact time the hanging would occur on the following day. My character, Prisoner E, began to take bets. My whole business lasted less than three minutes, but what joy I experienced during those three minutes. What rollicking good fun it was to be a part of *The Quare Fellow*!

There we were, twenty-two men cramped into a small dressing room. Except for one actor in his late thirties and another actor in his midsixties, who I later learned was clinically deaf, the rest of us actors were in our twenties. Innocent camaraderie filled that dressing room! We were supportive and childlike. We all knew it was a bad production and simply laughed at the occasion. This fostered a feeling of unity among us, a unity built on humor and goodwill. What we failed to produce on stage to serve the world of Brendan Behan's play, we captured backstage in the dressing room. And I made several drinking buddies to boot! There had been few experiences in my life that had brought me such joy and laughter as having been part of that most abominable production of *The Quare Fellow*. And to this very day, when the pressures of daily life ground their teeth upon my weary soul, I could recall some of those awful brogues or the butchering of Behan's prose, and without fail, there would come pouring from my mouth a hearty chuckle. Long live *The Quare Fellow*!

A few months after *The Quare Fellow* was laid to rest, I auditioned for a new theatre company in Manhattan on East Fourth Street between Avenues A and B. With his father signing the lease as guarantor, a gentleman named James Stein rented a space formerly owned by a diocese. Now it belonged to the city. When James took charge, the building was christened Rapp Arts Center. It looked more like a school auditorium than a theatre. A few days after my audition, James called me and asked me to join the company. The company consisted of both Equity and non-Equity actors. I was excited.

For his first production, James staged Bertolt Brecht's *Edward II* as an Actors' Equity—approved showcase. I was cast as the Abbot. James had a talented cast and a viable venue in a hip East Village.

Edward II bombed. *The Village Voice* reviewer referred to it as a "screaming mess." But I was in my twenties and acting in off-off-Broadway plays, and I didn't mind or notice if I was in terrible productions. I was working for nothing, but hungry for experience and stage-time. I was serious about my craft and wanted to grow. I was hopeful that I would be discovered by someone in the audience who could help my career along. I went from one turkey to another. I didn't care. I put into practice what I learned from Suzanne.

After *Edward II* closed, I stayed on. For the next production, I was cast as Andre in Anton Chekhov's *The Three Sisters*. It was another dud. The director attempted to stage the play as farce. The liveliest moment of the run came when a cat walked on stage during one of my scenes. I welcomed the moment. Without the slightest break in my character, I picked the cat up, crossed to an upstage door, opened it, and tossed the cat. The small audience roared with laughter. I believed I did the good Dr. Chekhov proud. After the final performance of *The Three Sisters*, my association with James Stein and his theatre company came to an end.

After departing from Rapp Arts Center, I resumed my place on the audition trail. In less than a month, I landed a role in an Equity-approved showcase of Tom Stoppard's *Dogg's Hamlet, Cahoot's Macbeth*, a pair of one-act plays. I played an English school lad cast as Juliet in his school's production of *Romeo and Juliet*. I auditioned for the role with Hamlet's short speech to the hired players that began, "Speak the speech I pray you, trippingly on the tongue…" I credit Suzanne for the refreshening of acting not only Shakespeare but also classical text in general.

One day in class, I was brushing up on a monologue of Benedick's from Shakespeare's comedy of manners, *Much Ado about Nothing*. I did the monologue once, and Suzanne said to me, "You speak very well, Larry. You speak almost too well. You're acting as though Benedick knows that Shakespeare wrote his part for him and that he should speak those wonderful words to make them sound oh so beautiful. Benedick never heard of Shakespeare." So true!

I performed in *Dogg's Hamlet, Cahoot's Macbeth* at the 1010 Players at 1010 Park Avenue in the basement of an Episcopalian church. The director sported a buzz cut and horn-rimmed granny glasses. She seldom spoke throughout rehearsals and performances. I was a bit lost. But I was gaining stage experience in an interesting repertoire of plays and continued honing my craft under Suzanne's aesthetically astute guidance.

Dogg's Hamlet, Cahoot's Macbeth closed at the end of March 1987. It had been three years and ten months since I graduated from Boston University's School of Theatre Arts. I was already a member of Actors' Equity Association and the Screen Actors Guild, and I had performed in nine stage plays. I determined to keep at it and continue to live the life.

During the years I waited tables, I was fired at least half a dozen times. I was fired from my very first job. It was the summer of '83, the very first summer the South Street Seaport opened for business in downtown Manhattan. I was hired at Steinhandler's Grill. I was twenty-two years old. I still lived at home with my parents in Roslyn, Long Island. When you're living at home with your parents, not needing to worry over rent or bills, what could beat ending a shift with eighty dollars in small bills cash fattening your wallet? A pint-sized Asian, Mr. Feng, managed Steinhandler's Grill. Mr. Feng turned out to be one of the more humane managers during my short reign as a waiter. One afternoon, a party of three left a three-dollar tip on a fifty-dollar check. My service was fine. A woman paid the check with a credit card. I asked why she left me "so small a tip on a fifty-dollar check." Mr. Feng witnessed this. He pulled me over and fired me on the spot. I learned later that if you receive an unduly small tip through no fault of your own, you could politely ask the patron if there was anything wrong with the service; if you were given the tip in cash with the amount due, you could return the cash tip to the table with a polite thank you.

I was never fired because of inept service; on the contrary, I was quite a capable waiter. More often I was fired because of a poor attitude toward management and a general unwillingness to kowtow to its authority. Sometimes I'd arrive to work in a creased collared shirt just to get a rise from my managers. I was fine with the customers. I recited the specials of the day with an understated flair. Yet I still loathed being a waiter and made no effort to hide this from my managers. I knew that I was made for better things than filling paper cups with coleslaw or folding cloth napkins or describing the contents of a relish tray or knowing the difference between tongue and pastrami—and not to mention donning an apron before my shift started.

I was able to adapt for the first couple of years because they were coupled with opportunities for me to shine on stage. But after the fifth year or so, I'd had enough. I reached the point where I was quietly reciting Shakespearean monologues while carrying plates to my customers.

A few weeks after the closing of *Dogg's Hamlet*, a casting director from CBS called me and cast me in the role of a gendarme in the daytime serial *Guiding Light*.

Guiding Light chronicled the travails of the family Bauer in Salem, Massachusetts. The narrative had temporarily shifted locales to Paris at the time I was cast as a gendarme. When I arrived at CBS studios in Chelsea at seven in the morning, I was instructed by the doorman to go downstairs to the green room. I was met there by a uniformed fellow gendarme, who informed me that a general assistant would soon arrive to greet us and let us in on the storyline. In the meantime, I changed into my gendarme garb.

When the general assistant arrived, we were told that there had been an art theft in a Parisian museum and that we gendarmes were in the museum to carry out some paintings. My fellow gendarme and I waited for two hours until someone announced through the green room's intercom for the gendarmes to report to studio C. My business consisted of silently carrying paintings in the background from one end of the set to the other while the main action took place in the foreground. It was all of four minutes' work. I was paid $125. It comes with a tinge of irony that my first television appearance had Paris as its setting and that, scarcely seven years later, I became a Francophile.

Some weeks after my *Guiding Light* gig, I received a phone call from Todd Thayler Casting. I was hired for two days of extra work on the Michael J. Fox vehicle *Bright Lights, Big City*, based on the Jay McInerney novel that I had read a few years back. We were shooting at the Tunnel Disco in Chelsea. I was a faceless body among a crowd of hundreds scattered in the background. I sensed a special kind of tension on the set. Sydney Pollack was the executive producer, and he was present. Joyce Chopra was the director, who had scored a critical success with *Smooth Talk*. It turned out that Joyce Chopra had been replaced by James Bridges and that my scenes had been scrapped from the finished product. By then, I was waiting tables at a Tex-Mex restaurant in midtown on the eastside, El Rio Grande. I continued studying with Suzanne.

In late March of 1988, I was cast in the role of James Strauss in Myer Levin's *Compulsion*. *Compulsion* is based on the Leopold and Loeb case, where two academically brilliant and privileged teens cold-bloodedly murdered a fourteen-year-old in the hope of having committed the perfect crime. James Strauss was the older brother of Artie Strauss, the younger of the two teenaged murderers. I, too, was an older brother, and like the character of James Strauss, I understood what it meant to have strained relations with my younger brother. It was a small role but one that needed a convincing performance to serve the world of the play.

Compulsion was produced by a friend of mine, Alec Harrington. I met Alec as fellow cast member in *The Quare Fellow*. Alec is the son of Michael Harrington, a founding member of the Democratic Socialists of America and author of *The Other America*, an examination of America's poverty class and required reading for those who served in the cabinet of the Kennedy administration. *Compulsion* was my tenth play and, thus far, the best acted and best directed. It was produced as an Actors' Equity—approved showcase, Alec managed to get some genuinely seasoned pros. *Compulsion* had a well-received twelve-performance run. Tony Award-winning actress Anne Wedgeworth attended a performance.

During the latter part of the run, I was fired from yet another waiter job. This was the first time I was accused of being rude to the customers. This occurred a few months after I was fired from El Rio Grande. I returned to the trail of finding another job waiting tables. I also applied to a catering company called Great Performances. A few days later, they gave me a call. They had a job for me. It would be temporary but would last at least a few weeks, and it paid ten dollars an hour—not a bad wage for unskilled labor in 1988. The job was located at John F. Kennedy Airport, in the cafeteria where luggage haulers had their meals. I bused and washed their dishes. My shift began at six in the morning. I had to be out of my door by four-thirty, first taking a subway then transferring to a bus.

I lasted a week. The cafeteria manager fired me because I arrived thirty minutes late for my shift without calling. I did call. I called as soon as got out of bed at five fifteen, realizing I had overslept. There was no answer in the manager's office. What was I to do but start on my way? After I was fired, I went home and called Great Performances, trying to appeal to them to ask the client for another chance. They said they were sorry, adding, "That's the kind of man the manager is." There I was, reading Sartre but couldn't hold down a dishwasher's job.

About a week later, I was hired to move office furniture for corporate businesses that were relocating. The Jersey-based company ran its operations from midnight to seven. I was the youngest member of the crew. Some crew members looked like they were addled by either drugs or alcohol, desperate for income. I was paid eight dollars an hour. I knew on the first shift that I would not last. I didn't have the back strength needed to move desks, swivel chairs, and file cabinets. Nor did I like the idea of going to bed at eight in the morning. After my first shift, I returned home and slept for five fours. Then I went in search of another job waiting tables.

I made my comeback to the restaurant business at Paparazzi, an Italian eatery at the corner of Fifty-Second Street and Second Avenue. Its corporate office was nearby. I liked the woman who interviewed me. She referred to Paparazzi as a family restaurant. Paparazzi had a quaint charm. The dishes were prepared in a partitioned kitchen right on the main dining room floor, where homemade pasta hung in sheets from rods. The silverware and glasses were cleaned downstairs, where they were sent through a dumbwaiter. I practiced my Spanish with the kitchen staff. When my customers' orders were ready, the head cook in the kitchen would ring the bell on the slide and affectionately call out, "Lencho!"

Soon after starting at Paparazzi, I lucked into some more extra work on the Richard Pryor/Gene Wilder comedy, *See No Evil, Hear No Evil*. It turned out to be a four-day gig. I was filmed in two scenes. The first three days were shot in the lobby of an office building near Union Square. Wilder played a deaf man who ran a newsstand. Pryor played an unemployed blind man.

After a production assistant escorted the extras to the set from the holding area, a second or third assistant director came over to the group and pointed to another male extra and me. "You and you, come with me," he said. We dutifully followed him to a spot in the lobby at a fair distance from the newsstand where Wilder and Pryor played their scene. The assistant director continued, "All right, guys, when we call action and the scene begins, I want you to talk to each other. What's your name?" he asked the other male extra.

"Robby."

"All right, Robby. After you and—what's *your* name?" he asked me.

"Larry."

The assistant continued talking to Robby. "About three to five seconds after you and Larry start talking, I want you to walk over to the newsstand and end up on Mr. Pryor's left. Here's some change." He handed Robby a few coins. "When you end up in front of the newsstand to Mr. Pryor's left, put the change on the counter and take a *New York Post* and come right back here."

"What do I do?" I asked.

He looked surprised at my question. The he turned, walked to the newsstand, grabbed a *New York Post*, returned to us, and said, "Here, Larry, read *The New York Post*."

During my other scene, when I was part of a stream of pedestrians walking by in the background of the principals, I talked with another male extra named Neil. During a break for lunch, Neil and I ate at a nearby Japanese restaurant. He turned out be a playwright currently working on what he referred to as "a film noir for the stage." Neil cast me in the role of David Breen, a principal part. I've forgotten the play's title and plot, but it was the first time I was killed on the stage and the only time I was to torture someone on stage. We had an eight- or nine-performance run at an armpit of a Black Box on lower Broadway (not to be confused with the Broadway in the Theatre District). The men's dressing room stank of bodily fluids. There was a sign leaning against a mirror that read: "Please do not leave food around. We have rats—big 'uns."

It was around the time that I started writing poetry. Most of it was nonsensical drivel. Some of it was self-deprecating confession. Some of it celebrated free form for free form's sake. It was a welcome release from the predictable pattern my life had taken—studying with Suzanne, acting in off-off-Broadway showcases of varying quality, waiting on tables. Though my poems lacked craft and were not the writings of a disciplined poet, hundreds poured from me. Beat poet Gregory Corso once told me of Jack Kerouac's pronouncement on the impulse to string sentences together on the page: "First thought, best thought." The late '80s saw a resurgence of interest in the Beat movement with the release of the documentary *Whatever Happened to Kerouac?* Many young people like me admired the Beats more for their Bohemian posturing than for the literary merit of their work. So like many a poet-poseur, I effortlessly fell into the role. I still have most of the poems I wrote. Of the thousands of lines I composed, one phrase would readily come to mind: "brew-stained wood."

Sometime in early spring 1989, I was fired from Paparazzi. Back then, restaurants were mostly using actors and others trying to break into the arts. It's different now. You still have the handsome waiter with dreams of stardom, but you also have a waiter who'd be perfectly satisfied being a waiter and staying a waiter. Restaurant owners can rest easier at night knowing this. But at the time of my demise from Paparazzi, there was still a very high turnover rate of waiters, and there were always jobs available. I was hired at the Boathouse in Central Park.

On a Sunday afternoon shift, I saw the owner lurking around the restaurant, up and down the aisles and in between tables. She wouldn't look at me or at any of the customers. She was just a self-contained presence. She probably witnessed my having words with the bartender, an oafish lout who took an immediate dislike to me. I stepped up to the service station at the end of the bar to get my customers' drinks, and though he knew I was waiting, he kept making small talk with the customers at the bar, sometimes folding his arms in the bargain. I called him on it. Then he became defensive and claimed he didn't appreciate my "attitude." When he started the next sentence, I interrupted by saying, "I'd love to stand here and keep hobnobbing with you, but I think a customer needs a refill." The owner probably witnessed this exchange. Or it could be that the bartended complained to her about me. I lasted a week at the Boathouse.

My next job waiting tables would be my last.

Zia was at the northeast corner of Eighty-Eighth Street and Second Avenue. It opened just a couple of months prior to my being hired. I worked dinner shifts along with the brunch shift. The one weekday lunch shift I worked was a virtual joke. I worked both the front and back dining rooms by myself. There was no busboy because there were never any customers for lunch. For some reason, Zia could not attract a lunch crowd. In the kitchen, there was only Sal, the line cook. Sal taught me the proper method of adding spices to food while I was cooking. You should always hold the spice shaker at least ten inches above the pot or pan. This would allow for a more even distribution of the granules over the food.

Things went along at Zia without incident. Then sometime in May, my father suggested that I give Tony Watson a call. Back in the midseventies, my father's public relation firm did some work for Tony's firm, Health Systems Agency, a federally funded watchdog group that monitored budgets and expenditures of city hospitals. Health Systems Agency was my father's own account. My father had a personal admiration for Tony because Tony held his own against Washington bureaucrats.

When I graduated from high school in June of '79, Tony got me a job in the Xerox room in the Queens office of Health Systems Agency. At the time, there was an HSA office in all five boroughs of the city of New York. Tony worked in the Manhattan office. During a few winter breaks in my undergraduate years, I worked in the HSA Xerox room in the Manhattan office, the only one left in the city. In the early winter of 1984, I went back to work in the Xerox room at

HSA, now located in a dingy office on lower Broadway. I wanted a break from waiting tables. In exchange for my modest wage, I had a sense of stability and a stress-free work environment. I left HSA in September of '84 and returned to waiting on tables, slinging plates of overstuffed sandwiches and scoops of potato salad at Applebaum's Delicatessen, right across the street from Pennsylvania Station.

I'd never really spoken to Tony Watson. I only glimpsed him a few times sitting behind his desk as I handed his mail to his secretary. Whenever I returned to work at HSA, I always dealt with someone in Human Resources. So I was utterly surprised that sunny spring morning in 1989 when I suddenly found myself alone with Tony, sitting by his side, in front of his desk, in his office at the headquarters of Health Insurance Plan of Greater New York (HIP), where Tony was the executive director.

We were both facing his desk. He put his fingertips together. Tony looked straight ahead and said, "Larry, it'll all fall into place."

What would fall into place? I thought. *My life? Life itself? And what did the great Anthony L. Watson Jr. really know about my life?* It was true that he knew that I was an actor. There were even a few staff members at HSA who came to see me perform in my only musical, *Allegro*, back in the spring of '84. My father told me that Tony told him that "some of our staff" had seen the play and got a real kick out of me "singin' and dancin' and all."

Yet I was still a virtual stranger to Tony. He might have known the surface of my life. Why was this busy and important man taking time out of his busy schedule to sit down with me? My father told me that Tony had a son around my age who had joined the Navy. Perhaps Tony was rehearsing with me before he sat down with his own son? Perhaps Tony wanted to know what it would feel like for the words to leave his lips in the actual presence of a man young enough to be his son before he spoke to his real son. I could only theorize until the cows came home.

At one point, I pronounced to him that I was a liberal.

"Well," he paternally responded, "we're a liberal organization, and at the same time, we try to help the community." Before I knew it, Tony had offered me a job, and I accepted.

"Hello, this is HIP's emergency medical services, Operator 208 speaking. How can I help you?" This was what I said each time a call came in. And on some shifts, there could be close to one hundred. I became an emergency medical coordinator. My first shift was the graveyard shift, from one in the morning until nine. The callers were all members of HIP.

HIP's emergency medical services began operations at five in the afternoon, when HIP medical clinics closed for the day. For instance, a young mother's nine-month-old son developed an alarmingly large rash on his thigh. Not knowing what to do, she called 1-800-HIP-HELP.

Then this golden voice (my voice) came through the line: "Hello, this is HIP'S emergency medical services, Operator 208 speaking. How can I help you?"

Then I'd take down her name, address, phone number, HIP identification number, the child's name, age, sex, and most importantly, the reason for the call. After ending the call, I'd put the information into a vertical slot. A designated "runner" for the hour would periodically empty the slot of incoming calls, bring them to an adjoining office, and place the information sheets on either a nurse's or physician's desk. The HIP member would receive a callback from the respective medical staffer and, depending on the degree of emergency, would be given advice or an urgent appointment at an HIP medical facility for the following day or a referral to the nearest emergency room.

The operators wore headsets attached to a microphone. Incoming calls were signaled by a beep. The amount and consistency of incoming calls depended on the shift you worked. The graveyard shift had the least. Peak hours would usually run from 6:00 p.m. until 8:00 p.m. There were periods when as soon as an operator ended a call, another would automatically come in. You could go from one call to another for a half an hour. That was probably my record without stopping. Calls could be monitored by the supervisor, as were the number of calls you were taking. An operator had the option to suspend incoming calls for a bathroom break, a cigarette, or a personal call. Most calls were not serious emergencies. The reason for the call could range from a runny nose to teething, a stomachache, chronic diarrhea, an earache, a sore throat, or a burning sensation while urinating.

There were calls referred to as a "direct connect." For instance, a call came in from someone over the age of thirty-five who complained of chest pains. In a case like this, the caller would be placed on hold and the operator would announce, "Direct connect!" Then the designated runner would take the information sheet from the operator, run it back to triage, and bring it to a physician. Once the physician had the information sheet in hand, the original operator would connect the caller to the physician. This process usually took less than a minute. There were a few other emergencies that merited direct connects: vaginal bleeding, shortness of breath, and dizziness.

But then there was my favorite call of all—the "psyche" call. "Psyche" callers could be those threatening suicide, recovering addicts on the verge of relapsing, anyone posing a threat to themselves or others, or anyone needing the assistance of the mental health doctor on call. I can't recall any training on how to precisely handle psyche calls other than never putting someone on hold who was threatening suicide. If an operator did receive a psyche call from someone threatening suicide, the runner would alert the supervisor, and the supervisor would then contact the mental health doctor on call and then conference the mental health doctor into the operator's line to speak to the at-risk caller.

The only psyche call I ever received came from a distraught woman calling from Staten Island. She told me that her husband was walking around the neighborhood, talking to himself. She said she was "frightened."

What are you frightened about? I thought. *Maybe your husband's evolving!*

On my second shift, which was 5:00 p.m. until 11:00 p.m., I began taking calls. Of the thousands of calls I received as an emergency medical coordinator at HIP, I most vividly remember my very first call. A woman was calling for her husband. She told me that her husband, a city bus driver, was bleeding from his rectum.

Poor man, I thought.

But then sympathy gave way to a sort of egoistic selflessness. This was certainly a new feeling for me, that of genuinely helping another human being out of a crisis. For the first time in my life, I felt I was doing important work. I was suddenly thrust into a reality stripped to its core. After the bus driver told his wife he was bleeding, I was the first person to be informed. How special I felt! Much more special than I ever felt taking a curtain call or being complimented on a performance. How needed I felt! What a far cry from the humiliation of donning an apron in restaurants and basically groveling for my living. Perhaps I self-dramatize as much now as I did when I took my first call at HIP, but there is a vast chasm that lies between servant and angel.

I was paid eleven dollars an hour, a respectable wage for 1989. I worked a twenty-hour workweek over three shifts. I divided my labor between HIP and Zia. At summer's midway, I was cast as Buckingham in an Equity-approved showcase of *Richard III*. A fellow classmate in Suzanne's class played Richard and self-produced it as well. There were a few other students in the production from Suzanne's class. *Richard III* ran for about a dozen performances at the Theatre at St. Clement's Church on West Forty-Sixth Street between Ninth and Tenth Avenue. And dear Suzanne attended a performance. After the performance, all of us kid actors swarmed around Suzanne like frolicking chicks at the feet of the mother hen.

In mid-August, my father called in a favor from his former English professor at Long Island University's downtown Brooklyn campus. His name was Dr. Robert Spector. He had since risen to chairmanship of the English Department. Dr. Spector arranged an interview for me with Dr. Barbara Pasternak, Chairperson of the Speech and Theater Department. Perhaps Dr. Pasternak owed Dr. Spector a favor. My father told me there might be a course in public speaking that I could teach at LIU and that Barbara Pasternak wanted to talk to me about it. Our talk lasted less than five minutes. Perhaps I had the position before I walked in the door. Dr. Pasternak told me to return to the campus in a couple of days to pick up a copy of the textbook in my mailbox.

When I returned, there was a note enclosed between the text's flap and first page. It read, "Here's the textbook, Larry. Here's the real challenge."

This puzzled me. What "challenge" was she referring to? I hardly thought that teaching public speaking to a group of undergraduates constituted a challenge. Playing the part of a gay wrestler who kissed and hugged his lover throughout the play—*that* was a challenge. I read the first three chapters of the textbook, *The Art of Public Speaking*, and its instructive methodology seemed simple and straightforward enough. I wasn't nervous at all—until I stepped into the classroom on my very first day.

It was a class of fifteen students, an ideal size for a basic skills course. All the students were Black. No problem there. My roommate during my freshman year at Boston University was Black. My one and only good friend during my senior year was Black. When I worked in the mailroom at HSA, the other workers in the mailroom were Black, as most of the staff members were. When I worked at HIP, most operators were Black. Yet the moment I stepped into that classroom, my heartbeat quickened, a serpent began to coil at the base of my abdomen, my mouth began to dry, and my hands began to shake. I had been nervous before making my stage entrances throughout high school and college and for my first few productions in Manhattan. But what actors called stage nerves was not so much nervousness but a welcomed adrenalin rush. If the actor was of any genuine caliber, within moments of his entrance, he would embrace the world of the play. And there was the imaginary fourth wall that separated the actor from the audience. There was no such "fourth wall" in the classroom.

All eyes were on me, and I had to produce my own schema. I sucked back my cheeks and I mumbled, "Good morning." A few students responded in kind. I turned and took a seat behind the desk. I proceeded to share my thoughts on the importance on speech communication, how better communication could help our relationships, and how mastering the art of public speaking could expand a college graduate's marketability for employment. My words came directly from the heart. I believed the students appreciated my sincerity, spontaneity, vulnerability. They knew I was nervous. Perhaps they felt empowered? Did I win them over because of this?

The class ran for seventy-five minutes. I filled the first hour with a lecture and used the remaining fifteen to go over the syllabus. By that time, my heartbeat slowed, the serpent uncoiled, my salivary glands began to secrete at their normal output, and my hands steadied. I dismissed the class on a note of confidence and anticipation of what lay in store. Some of the students smiled at me as they made their way to the door. One of them stayed behind and approached my desk.

"Hello," I said.

"Hello."

"What's your name again?" I was terrible at remembering names then—and I continue to be.

"Raymond."

"Can I help you?"

"Can I talk to you?" he asked.

"Yes."

"I can't talk now. I have a class. How about later?"

"Fine. Come to the fourth floor to the Speech and Theater Department. When's a good time for you?"

"How about an hour and a half?"

"Perfect," I said.

I used an office that was normally occupied by a tenured professor who was on sabbatical.

It turned out that Raymond needed counsel on how to handle a family matter. It was his father. All his father seemed to be doing with himself was lying around the house and drinking. I told Raymond he could contact Al-Anon or Alcoholics Anonymous. I didn't feel comfortable asking Raymond any further questions about his father's drinking or the rest of his family. I was not sure if I was any help at all, but Raymond never mentioned the matter again. What puzzled me was why he approached me about it in the first place. He'd known me an hour and fifteen minutes. Perhaps I appeared to be approachable, good-natured, attentive, personable, and nonjudgmental. And I wasn't much older than Raymond. I suppose Raymond wanted an audience with a nice person in a position of authority. I never really found out why he chose me. But on that very first day of class, I talked about communication as it related to our personal as well as professional lives. For whatever reason Raymond approached me, I'd surely made a favorable impression without even trying.

By the third class, I completely relaxed into my new role. I was playing the role of professor and was loving every second of it. Whether or not my students were retaining the information after leaving the class was an entirely different story. My lectures and class discussions were lively and honest, and of course, the fact that I used my voice and body in a highly theatrical manner helped a lot. It was a highly unsuitable use of the voice and body for the stage, unless you were a glazed ham sitting in a deli's window. But for the classroom, it worked to the audience's benefit, especially in a course the students were required to take. I wasn't declaiming to the heavens with grand gestures, just enjoying words and enjoying the fact that my students enjoyed watching *me* enjoy myself.

This is what's referred to in communications argot as emotional contagion. If the person sending the verbal message is enthused of the content and the enthusiasm is displayed through voice, body, and gesture, the message will more likely land on receptive ears. Some parents mouth the words of a bedtime story to their child, while other parents enliven the story, making occasional eye contact with their child. Are these the lucky children who will perhaps dream the story soon after their heads touch the pillow and their night lamps are turned off?

I loved being in front of a class. I was actor, director, and playwright all in one. I never sat down. Nor did anyone need suggest that it was engaging for me to walk up and down the aisles in between the rows of chairs. Audience involvement. My wages stood at $1,400, which was way below the national median for a three-credit course taught by an adjunct. That didn't bother me. I was more excited that I found a trade besides theatre that I enjoyed. It was a trade that tapped my abilities, my creativity, a trade with a high degree of autonomy, a trade wherein I could bring forth my personality.

While Long Island University's wage for an adjunct was low, there was another problem. For a fifteen-week semester, I received three checks. My first check arrived in the mail in mid-October. The second check arrived the week after Thanksgiving. My final check arrived a week after I submitted my final grades. A university's appropriated funds for adjuncts' wages could sit in the bank and collect more interest than dust. Many adjuncts teach at more than one college during a given semester. Some adjuncts do so to survive. Some adjuncts do so for the perks that come from additional income. Some adjuncts are retirees from the public school system. There are some adjuncts who teach one or two courses a couple of afternoons a week at one college while their mothers or hired nannies look after their toddlers. There are adjuncts who are unwed mothers who hold PhDs and live just above the poverty level. Some adjuncts are twentysomething graduate students living at home in a grand manor with their mommy and daddy. And then there is a special kind of adjunct. They are well established and reputable in their chosen professions: dentistry, law, criminal justice, medicine, architecture, engineering, and any of the fine or popular arts.

For instance, a high-powered contract attorney had just been saddled with draconian child support and alimony. Why not sniff out an adjunct position teaching contract law a couple of nights a week to help with your monthly payments? Or, for example, an NYPD homicide detective wanted to take his new girlfriend to Paris to show her how cultured and world-travelled he was. Why not teach a course in forensics at John Jay College of Criminal Justice of the City University of New York? These chosen few could demand and receive a much higher wage than a common adjunct, especially if they were teaching on the graduate level and especially if they'd made a name for themselves in their chosen fields. These adjuncts do not make their living as adjuncts, so any wage is extra income. The retired public school teacher could afford a modest wage because he's receiving a handsome pension. It appeared that certain administrators at Long Island University assumed that their adjunct faculty had other means of adequate financial support, either from other educational institutions or entirely from other professions.

I fell into the latter. I still worked a twenty-hour week at HIP and waited tables a few evenings a week at Zia. I also roomed with my brother. We shared a one-bedroom unit, and because I kept later hours, I slept on the living room couch. I paid a little over $400 a month for rent. Zia had opened the previous spring. It had a successful weekend turnover, especially when it added outdoor dining. But after Labor Day, business fell. After the first week of October, when management discontinued outdoor dining, business plummeted. I gave management a week's notice on October 24th. I ended a thoroughly undistinguished career as a waiter on Halloween 1989.

Naturally, I'm very pro-Labor. I don't mean to say that Labor is always right in their demands and that the management is unjust in denying said demands. What I mean to say is that work is important, especially when applied to youth. Flipping burgers, scooping ice cream, and spooning coleslaw into plastic cups certainly lack nourishment for the brain, but as Dr. King so wisely noted, "There is dignity in all labor." That might be difficult for the young to embrace.

Speaking for myself, I felt a greater sense of dignity washing dishes in a Greek restaurant than I did a nervous and insecure teenager walking the halls of Roslyn High School. And of course, now more than ever, working in your teens can have immeasurable value to your intercultural communication skills. You might very well meet people your own age but of different ethnicity and race and with different problems or concerns they might be willing to share with you. I'd had many part-time and some full-time jobs that I didn't particularly like. But in all of them, I felt some sense of dignity and self-worth, and I learned things about myself as well as of others. I'm eternally hopeful that I could say the same of my six years waiting on tables. But on that October 31st Halloween night in 1989, while walking down Second Avenue, those masks of goblins, witches, and deformed netherworld creatures were anything but grotesque. Never had I been able to see such beauty in ugliness.

On the morning that followed my final bow to waiting tables, I felt particularly jubilant in class. The lesson fell to concrete versus abstract language in verbal expression. I had previously encouraged the students to purchase a copy of *Roget's Thesaurus* as an introduction to the range of adjectives available in English. Then the discussion evolved to how certain adjectives possessed multiple usages. The class and I constructed the following list: *cool, neat, oily, fine, cheap, dirty, kosher, stiff, rich, poor, high, low, blue, green, yellow,* and *wooden.* We explored how these words could be assigned both a literal and figurative meaning.

"You can toss your salad with wooden utensils."

"There are certain movie actors with formidable physiques, but their performances are wooden."

"Green is the predominant color on American paper currency."

"He's a good surgeon but too green for triple bypass surgery."

Then the lesson moved to homonyms and homophones, which I learned of from a slim study of the English language I borrowed from the campus library.

"I never met a nun that liked me."

"I'll have none of your sarcasm."

"I'm just a humble patrolman who walks a neighborhood beat."

"I can't peel any more potatoes. I'm beat."

"I will not marry you unless you slip a ring on my finger."

"Sometimes you're so smart I'd like to ring your neck."

"Peace on earth and good will toward all."

"Hey, Grandma, can I have another piece of your kidney pie?"

Oliver Twist said, "Please, sir… I want some more."

"It's rather difficult to farm on a windswept moor."

"Don't think of Othello as simply a shade of Black. He was more than that."

"Think of him as Othello the Moor!"

I was reappointed for the spring semester at LIU.

PART II

BY THE SEA

Sometime after the first of the year, I was speaking with a Dr. Mortimer Becker in his office in the Western Cluster of Kingsborough Community College of the City University of New York. The Aspen Institute College Excellency Program ranked KCC among the top four community colleges in the nation. Dr. Becker chaired the Department of Communication and Performing Arts. From what little time I spent in his office, I concluded that I was in the presence of a true gentleman. When I attended Dr. Becker's ceremonial dinner some months after my interview, one of the department's secretaries referred to his "quiet dignity."

One day, about halfway into the spring semester, I went to the Department of Communications and Performing Arts to check my mail. Dr. Becker emerged from his office. When he hired me, it was his last semester before retiring. During my first semester at KCC, Dr. Becker still used his office, but he already named a Dr. Cliff Hesse as the new chairman. After Dr. Becker emerged from his office, he smiled at me and, with the wave of his hand, gave me a lyrically dismissive gesture. On hindsight, I interpret this gesture to mean that I was way too young and clueless to really understand mortality. I think that when he made the gesture, he knew he didn't have a long time left in this world. Dr. Becker died a few months later.

I was referred to Dr. Becker by Dr. Spector at LIU. I believe that during our interview, Dr. Becker was evaluating and assessing me, trying to sense if I had the strengths needed to teach a public speaking course at a reputable community college. At LIU, Dr. Pasternak just wanted to meet and make sure I was a well-spoken young man. I very much liked Dr. Becker. He made me feel welcomed. Mind you, I still tasted ash in my mouth from waiting tables and working in tense environments. Perhaps you can understand why I was so impressed by Dr. Becker's gentleness and "quiet dignity." When one works for curt and cold managers, one can tend to overappreciate plain humanity.

When I sensed the conclusion of my interview with Dr. Becker, I asked him, "So can I teach a course for you?"

"I'll give you two. Come with me."

He stood, came around from behind his desk, and made a gesture befitting a nobleman that parlayed that I was to lead the way. He certainly had a way of gesturing, Dr. Becker did. When he followed me out of his office, he placed his hand on my shoulder and said to his secretary, "Larry will be joining our adjunct faculty." Then he turned to me. "Like to fill out the paperwork now?"

"Of course."

Then Dr. Becker nodded to his secretary, cuing her to begin the process.

This was style!

"Welcome to Kingsborough," his secretary said. And she meant it. She was a sweet elderly woman. There was another elderly secretary in the office who was just as sweet. I have since come to learn that among faculty and administration in academia, sweetness can be a welcomed surprise; eccentricity, a find for the ages. A cool and distant politeness is the norm.

I've always regretted not having the opportunity to get to know Dr. Becker. I suppose I could have learned a good deal from him about a great many things. He was the kind of man who, if you poked your head in his door and asked to see him about something, he would stop whatever he was doing and give you his time. Dr. Becker's replacement, Dr. Cliff Hesse, was no different. A good man was chosen by a good man. Prior to attending Dr. Becker's ceremonial dinner, I had been notified that I was scheduled for an observation. An observation was customary for adjunct faculty, and a full-time tenured faculty member would sit in on your class and observe. I had never been observed at LIU. I was petrified.

At Dr. Becker's ceremonial dinner, Dr. Hesse said to me, "An observation is nothing to worry about. It's just an opportunity to evaluate you and point out your strengths and some weaknesses."

I thought carefully before responding, "Worrying is in my blood."

Doctor Hesse's tall frame keeled over while he shook with silent laughter. And Cliff's sense of humor could be self-deprecatory. Self-deprecatory humor is a hard find anywhere, yet Cliff had it in spades.

One day I was sitting in the department's office, talking to one of the secretaries. Cliff was on the phone in his office. He listened more than he spoke. When he did speak, it was only to say either "I see" or "Okay" or "I understand." He uttered short sentences possessing compounds like *subcommittee* or *senate subcommittee* and other forms of bureauspeak. He seemed quite disinterested. Cliff had quite the prepossessing voice. He had a professional background in broadcasting. A few moments after ending his call, he emerged from his office, looked at the floor, and ran his index finger up and down over his lips while vocalizing. I've sometimes felt like doing that after attending some department meetings and listening to academic mumbo jumbo. I could well imagine the bureaucratic babble coming from the other end of Cliff's line.

It's one thing having trouble understanding or digesting information that's at bottom worthwhile, like physics or epidemiology. But trying to wrap your mind around the driest of information that constitutes the basis of rigid institutional infrastructure can numb your brain. Understanding the bureaucratic underpinnings of an academic institution is part of a chairperson's responsibility, and there are many meetings—meetings that can cover the most tiresome of topics.

Should XYZ remain the prerequisite to the QRS course? Should we implement an alternative prerequisite? Or should there be a departmental exam that should be passed in addition to fulfilling the XYZ coursework before the students can enroll in the QRS course? These kinds of profound and earth-shaking questions can put a preternaturally hyperactive methamphetamine addict under the deepest of slumbers. There's usually a vote on such questions. Then there's a call for a second motion. What should normally take five minutes to arrive at an answer to a question of policy can take academics twenty-five minutes. It could be because academics have notions of meeting a deadline that can differ from the usual corporate mindset.

There are many instances when a chairperson is sitting in his or her chair because no one else wanted the job. There are many chairpersons who aren't even full professors. Sometimes they're assistant professors. A chairmanship is a job that calls for an administrator as well as an educator. Administration calls for the application of regimentation and regulation with little to no room for imagination.

Many fine and creative professors won't go near a chairmanship. But a chairmanship yields a greater salary than a professorship, and there might exist opportunities to strengthen and expand the department. You can add courses to the department's curriculum. Maybe you teach for an English Department, and you think the current course offerings are hackneyed and that the literature fails to address the concerns or the experiences of the students. When you step in as chairman, you propose a course called Literature and the Working-Class Experience. In the course description, you include such authors as Upton Sinclair, James Farrell, Raymond Carver, and Charles Bukowski. This course has a fine chance of being approved because, at this college, many students are from working-class families. You somehow know in your bones that the young men in this college can better relate to Studs Lonnigan than Ahab.

Your proposal is accepted by a budget committee, and Literature and the Working-Class Experience is offered for the very first time. There is one section. You need at least twelve students to register for the course to run. The term begins, and there are only ten students registered, but you're granted an extra week to allow students to register late. On the second week of class, you reach the required number as you see four new faces. You give the course your all, and you know that the students are enjoying it because they're attending the class regularly, embracing your message, and asking questions; everyone remains in the course.

You know there's a definite possibility the students are thinking about the course when they are not in class because, through readings and class discussions, they are learning some of the unspoken shadings that can mark a life spent in the occupation of physical labor. And the students can internalize this because many of them have witnessed working-class lives first-hand. The students who take your course relate an enthusiastic word to other students.

Literature and the Working-Class Experience is offered a second semester, but this time, there are twenty-three students enrolled, plus another five who are registered late. In only one semester, your class size doubles. You know that you have been successful because Literature and the Working-Class Experience is an elective as opposed to a required course.

An encouraging word-of-mouth has spread. Now, as you approach the third semester that your baby is offered, you propose to a different committee that another section be added. The committee reviews the numbers, and your proposal to add another section is approved. You are leaving a personal mark on the English Department since taking over the chairmanship.

On my second semester at KCC, the Department of Communications and Performing Arts offered a new course called Sports Journalism. I briefly met the newly hired adjunct who wrote a sports column for a Brooklyn weekly. Alas, the course ran for only one semester. I think it was Cliff Hesse's idea to create the course. There were only two other instances I witnessed a new course offered. The second instance occurred a few semesters later. The course was called the Golden Age of Radio. I taught it. I felt comfortable discussing the medium of radio as a social and political force in America. I felt very comfortable talking about how radio introduced classical music to the millions of Americans who lived beyond the reach of a concert hall. I called this an example of a democratization of an art form. I felt extremely comfortable talking about Orson Welles's *Mercury Theatre*. I did not feel comfortable talking about such figures as Burns and Allen, Jack Benny, Bob Hope, Arthur Godfrey, Edgar Bergen, Kate Smith, or any other popular entertainer whose career began in radio before transitioning to television. I was a late baby boomer. But many of my students were alive back then and remembered listening. Many of them were local retirees who were filling time.

The first time I mentioned Jack Benny, an old red-haired woman raised her hand and said, "Whenever I hear the name Jack Benny or see him on TV reruns, I always think about rice pudding."

"Why?" I asked.

"Whenever my mother and I listened to Jack Benny in the kitchen, we'd always eat rice pudding."

The other instance a course was offered for the first time, it was only my third semester teaching at Mercy College. Paul Trent, the coordinator of the Media Division, knew my background and had enough faith in me to offer the opportunity to teach the Hollywood Western, which turned out to be somewhat of a bumpy ride along the trail.

My first semester at KCC passed like a dream. It was spring, and I was teaching by the sea. My two sections of Public Speaking were large: thirty plus students in each. How could I mind? They were listening. Very early in the semester (it could have been the first day of class), I was lecturing on the expectations and differences of a public speaking course compared to other college courses.

I gestured with a clawed-shaped right hand when using the word *cower*, and I said, "In most college courses, a student just cowers in the background to the whims of the professor. But in this class, you can take center stage and teach me should the spirit move you."

Then a young woman raised her hand. "I understand what you're saying," she said. "But right now I'm hanging on every word you say, and I don't know how I can possibly achieve the same thing when I would get up in front of the class to speak."

I was wearing a suit. I was boyish. I scarcely looked much older than most of my students, but most importantly, I was able to use my voice and body to good effect. And this occurred instinctively. Some years later, these behavioral qualities were brought to my attention in a post-observation meeting.

Dave Frankel said to me, "And you're really the only one around here who knows how to use your voice and body."

The fun I was having was contagious. I don't wish to give the impression that, at this point, teaching for me served solely as an excuse to swagger into a classroom and wax pseudo-educational theory. I liked using the space and using my voice, varying its rate, pitch, and inflection. I was taught by a master—Daisette McKelvie. Daisy was my Voice and Diction instructor on my freshman year at Boston University. Besides Suzanne Shepherd, Daisy was the only other teacher I ever had who made a lasting difference.

Though I brought a distinctively instinctive vocal technique to my class lectures and discussions, they were fueled by academic content. I rigorously prepared for each class. I carefully read the chapters. I wrote out entire chapters from the textbook onto lined paper. I outlined the copied information onto index cards that I'd refer to (if needed) during my classes. I earned the bravura of my classroom delivery. Mind you, the rigor of my preparation stemmed more out of insecurity than dedication.

I better damn well sound like I know what I'm talking about, I'd constantly say to myself as I walked the halls of KCC that very first semester. I found a livelihood besides acting that I liked and allowed me to channel my abilities. At KCC—CUNY, I was paid well, received health benefits, and worked on a verdant campus where, after a late afternoon class, you could dip your toes in salt water. I felt supported by Cliff Hesse and my colleagues. I still had dreams of a career in the theatre, but I felt that the best possible alternative was teaching at the university level.

The year 1989 was a good time to begin teaching. This was before our source of portable amusement became a collective epidermic outgrowth. Walkmans had been the rage for a good seven years and were now giving way to Discmans. Many students walked the halls of KCC and LIU while grooving to the music coming through their headphones. But that was where it ended. Their headphones would be shed and their devices placed in a handbag or backpack before they entered my class. These students were aware enough and still possessed a degree of manners and propriety to realize that a classroom was no place for a portable device that served for no other purpose than amusement. I could walk into a class and make meaningful eye contact with students. They could have been thinking about what they learned from the previous class or the lesson to be covered in the present class.

It's interesting to note how these students had so fewer information outlets as do todays' students, yet they were a better brand of student. They had a wider attention span, were more focused, more reachable, more educable, and more likely to digest information and upgrade it to knowledge. Today, for every student who might hang on every word, there could be twenty thinking about whom to text once class was over or what to post to their Facebook page. This is a glib generalization but not entirely untrue. I sincerely hope for the future of the republic's citizenry that a student's portable wireless device is not as menacing competitor for the professor of medicine, law, engineering, or dentistry.

I always ask students to put their mobile devices away and out of sight when I begin class. They prefer to have their mobile devices on their desks while class is in progress. I find something frightful in this picture. Am I being too sensitive? Am I taking the position of power granted to me too seriously? Or is it perhaps the actor in me taking offense at the division of focus in my audience? I'm sure the frustration I've been feeling isn't new. I'm sure a political science professor would have preferred her students talking about Stalin or NATO during moments before class rather than the latest episode of *I Love Lucy*. And I'm sure my father would have rather seen me reading books or newspapers than watching television. One thing is for certain, during my years of public and college education, television sets were left at home.

Sometime late in the semester, I received my first in-class observation.

You received at least two weeks' notice. That gave me plenty of time to prepare a stellar lesson down to the letter. After the observation, I would have to schedule a meeting with my observer for her to point out both my strengths and weaknesses. The evaluation would be categorized, and for each category, I would be rated on a scale of poor to excellent. Some of the categories included classroom management, knowledge of subject matter, engagement with students, prompt start of the lesson, professional appearance, clarity of voice, volume, and encouragement of student participation. I would be given an overall rating for the entire class and would either be recommended or denied a reappointment for the following semester. And the observer could also write a commentary.

I was observed by an elderly woman. She began our meeting by stating how much she liked my tie. I'd forgotten the content of the lesson, but I received either good or excellent in the subcategories and a good for the overall lesson. I was offered reappointment for the fall.

For fall 1990, my course load consisted of one Public Speaking course at LIU and one Public Speaking course and one Remedial English course at KCC. This was a time when both the senior and junior colleges at CUNY offered remediation in Math and English. Most of my students in Remedial English were non-native English speakers. The course used a workbook with exercises. The workbook was the brainchild of two full-time professors at KCC. Both were elderly women, both warm and likable. The workbook's title was *Listening and Speaking*, a user-friendly olio of roots, grammar, standard pronunciation. I immediately took to the material.

I loved learning Greek and Latin roots. I loved the interchanging of roots, like *philology* and *philanthropy*, *democracy* and *epidemic*, *autocracy* and *theocracy*. I felt privileged to learn that if you etymologically analyzed the word *pornography*, you could deduce that the very first form of pornography in Western culture was the writing of harlotry. I loved learning the meaning of prefixes and how suffixes determined a word's part of speech.

Most of all, I loved learning the diacritic alphabet. An entry in the dictionary is followed by parenthesized diacritic symbols. If an entry is polysyllabic, the diacritic symbols also possess stress marks. Each symbol represents a sound. These diacritic symbols serve as a guide for the reader to correctly pronounce the chosen word. That's how I learned how to pronounce *inchoate*.

So as the students learned the diacritic alphabet and its function, they honed their pronunciation skills. Learning the diacritic alphabet was of quite the service to me, as it gave me the tools to teach Voice and Diction, which was a course for non-native speakers that focuses exclusively on standard pronunciation of English. The alphabet that I used when teaching Voice and Diction was called the International Phonetic Alphabet (IPA). Throughout the years, I'd made use of the IPA in private tutorials.

Remedial English and Math has long been eliminated from the CUNY curriculum, thanks to former mayor Rudolph Giuliani. He believed remediation to be unnecessary for a student reaching the level of higher education, especially at institutions operating on public money. CUNY was dependent on state funding. Its budget could fluctuate from different gubernatorial and mayoral administrations. Academic programs' budgets could be slashed, thereby reducing the number of sections offered for any given course. For a fall semester, there could be twenty sections offered in Psychology 101. The following spring, the number of offered sections could be cut to ten.

Full-time faculty were contractually assured a certain number of courses per semester. They never felt a budget squeeze. Adjuncts did. There was little job security for CUNY adjuncts. We received a highly competitive wage, incremental wage increases, and eligibility for comprehensive health-care coverage, but our course loads could be reduced or could dissolve altogether with little to no notice. And some of us worked hard and received stellar observations in the bargain. That was why I never joined the Professional Staff Congress, the union that represented CUNY adjuncts. If I could receive the perks and benefits without paying dues, why should I bother? And PSC automatically ate ten dollars from every paycheck.

At the end of August '90, I gave notice at HIP. For the following fall semester, I taught two courses at LIU and two courses at KCC. I continued living with my brother and lived quite the modest lifestyle. The novelty of working at an Emergency Medical Hotline had long worn off.

Cliff Hesse observed my Remedial English class. In addition to the workbook used as an instructional guide, I also used the third-edition hardcover *Miriam Webster's New World Dictionary*. When a student griped at the thought of carrying such a heavy book to class, I replied, "Think of it as academic exercise."

The day Cliff observed me, the lessons of the day were adjective-forming suffixes, the differences between the comparative and superlative in adjectives, and the differences between slang and standard usage. The class and I used the dictionary as a reference point. Cliff brought a dictionary to class as he knew the lesson plans beforehand. Cliff sat in the far corner, his attention alternating between the dictionary and me. Toward the end of the class, I noticed that when he looked at me, he smiled, close-lipped and proud, as a father might smile from the bleachers while watching his son strike out batters on the Little League baseball field.

When class ended and the students left, Cliff approached my desk.

"Good lesson," he said.

"When shall we meet?" I asked.

"Can you come by my office in a couple of hours?"

"Yes."

"I'll see you then."

We shook hands.

When I later arrived in his office, Cliff opened the meeting by saying, "You're so darn articulate."

I received an excellent for the overall rating. My weaknesses were the following: Try not to turn my back so much to the class. Try not to allow a late student to disrupt my focus. Try to engage some of the shyer students.

Cliff suggested some tips to strengthen my weaknesses, and I thanked Cliff for his constructive criticism.

"Not at all," he said. "Keep up the good work."

By spring of '91, my excitement for teaching began to pale. I still enjoyed it very much and still rigorously prepared for my lessons, but now I began to look more objectively at the students' work in my Public Speaking classes. It became painfully clear to me how so few students excelled at public speaking. I wrestled with the causes. When I began teaching at better colleges, I discovered the reason. It was the brand of students I had. It was not that once I began teaching at better colleges with higher standards for admission, I was suddenly in the presence of students who had gifts for public address or truly embraced the art of oratory; they were simply better prepared for college. Most of my Hofstra University students had a superior public education compared to my Long Island University students.

The better public education one had received, the more equipped they were to handle college-level work and college-level expectations. One would have stronger written and verbal skills. I'd had students who were products of some of the lesser New York City public schools. Could that have been the reason for remediation at CUNY? A Hofstra University student was better prepared for college than a student from a poor performing inner city school, but there was one fact that united the two—neither of them had ever taken a Public Speaking class. Both students could come to me either terrified or indifferent at the prospect of having to deliver presentations in front of their peers. Both types of students had been shortchanged by the state in the state's quest for sustaining the status quo.

Since the fall of '91, on the first day of the semester, I'd always asked the students how many of them had ever taken a public speaking class or a basic oral communications class. I could count on my fingers the few times hands had been raised. Why was this so? What would happen if the art of public speaking were introduced to the American public-school pupil? And what would be the most appropriate age to introduce it? The earlier, the better.

Say we begin to introduce public speaking to sixth graders—nothing too complex. We have them report on a current event or an important historical event in American history or an important historical event in their native culture. Make it a requirement of the school curricula. Some of these sixth-grade students will probably hate it; some can take it or leave it. Some may also like it; some may even love it. One of the more important provisions to the success of this curricular innovation is the necessity for the teachers to give positive feedback.

The point is not to criticize the work of the students who are engaged by public speaking. The point is to validate and support their work. Make the students aware of how talented they are at public speaking and how interesting they are to listen to. This lays the foundation for the students to continue in the discipline on a voluntary basis as they advance in age. Then the teachers can raise their expectations and begin delineating the nuances of the art form. The goal is to have a core group of young men and women entering high school who are serious and confident in their ability to hold their audience's attention and either inform or persuade.

Sometime during the cultivation of the students' development in oratory, the ability of leadership should be mentioned. If you know that your words can hold the interest of a group of people, this will tap the self-confidence to lead others. The possible results of creating this core group of young people are endless. I believe that it will encourage more people to pursue community activism. This is already Emersonian in its embrace of self-reliance. Doesn't the state want to see poor neighborhoods improve?

As I write these very words, there may be young men or women walking their neighborhood streets and wishing they have the public verbal skills to give voice to the depth of their frustration with community conditions or their anger at their local municipalities. If more people have excellent public speaking skills, many things may begin to change.

There might be more ideas strewn on the national stage. More people would attend town meetings. The Labor community would have a more dynamic dialogue. Union representatives would be able to take a stronger stand when confronting management. Perhaps women's rights, gay rights, transgender rights, child advocacy, and the rights of the disabled would find stronger voices in articulating the needs of their respective movements. More people would be inclined to pursue public life in civil causes. And let's not forgot about the lobbyists representing special interest groups and corporate thuggery. That would level the playing field. And perhaps there might be an increase of those envisaging their opening statements to the men and women of the jury. Ay, could that be the first nub?

Uncle Sam houses enough counselors of law in his halls of justice. There also lies the threat of demagoguery. Some mush-mouthed, narcissistic, power-mad opportunist could come along and rally a mob. He could stand behind a podium in pursuit of our nation's highest office, spouting the most hollow of piecemeal platitudes. He could tap the reserves of envy, distrust, and suspicion, ever widening the already-existent racial divide. But we scarcely need the implementation of public speaking in our schools' curriculum to witness this.

At the completion of spring semester '91, I returned to working as a medical emergency coordinator at HIP. Adjuncts could consider themselves very lucky if they were offered courses during the summer term. Many academic departments shut down for the summer, and if your department remained active for the summer, the few courses running would more than likely be offered to adjuncts with more seniority than you had. I was out of a job. I vowed never to wait on tables after Halloween night in '89, so I returned to HIP.

"Good afternoon. This is HIP, Operator 208 speaking. How can I help you?"

That sure beat approaching a table and saying, "Good evening. Can I get you something from the bar?"

Like Kingsborough Community College, Brooklyn College was gated and enclosed from the din of the metropolis. You could sit on mowed grass under a sickly-looking oak and read your Baudelaire. Brooklyn College was in the Flatbush section, the last stop on the number 2 train.

I began teaching at Brooklyn College in the fall of '91. Long Island University was my father's alma mater. Brooklyn College was my mother's alma mater. And as Dr. Pasternak referred me to Kingsborough, Dr. Hesse referred me to Brooklyn College. Why was I being shunted around from university to university? Surely not for poor performance. Was it a time when a thirst for young blood in the classroom took hold? Or did Dr. Pasternak and Dr. Hesse appreciate and sympathize with the precariousness and lack of security in an adjunct's life and decide to do whatever was possible to ensure me a stronger foothold in the academic community? A sounder reason would be that the system came under an executive directive to use as many adjuncts whenever and wherever possible. Adjuncts were recognized as cheap labor, hungry for work, and willingly exploitable. The dye had been cast. We had arrived. We were money savers for the universities, we adjuncts. Why hire full-time tenure-track professors when you could receive equal or even better-quality teaching for a pittance?

Many students at Brooklyn College were Orthodox Jewish. The chairman of the Speech Department, Dr. Charles Parkhurst, was Jewish. The department's secretary was Jewish. I particularized her Jewishness in perceiving her as a Jewish mother, which was not too difficult to do when you were raised by one.

The department's secretary took a shine to me.

"Don't you look nice," she'd say.

Another time, she said, "You're so thin. Doesn't your mother feed you?"

I replied, "Only when I let her. If I'm not careful, she'll have me in the highchair again, spooning me strained peas."

To this, the secretary replied, "Only if she strained them herself."

Another time, she asked me, "Have you eaten in the cafeteria yet?"

"No."

"Try the scrod. They serve it every Wednesday and Friday."

I took her advice and tried the scrod. It was watery, limp, garnished by a soggy lemon.

A few weeks later, the secretary asked, "So did you ever try the scrod?"

"Yes, I did, and I have to say—"

"I know. Isn't it terrible? I keep asking myself, how could anyone make scrod taste like that? Can you tell me?"

I taught one course at Brooklyn College. I also taught one course at KCC and one course at LIU, and I continued working two nights a week at HIP. I was a young man with energy to burn. I also taught a few mornings a week at an armpit of a facility called Techno-Dent Training Center. This was a trade school that taught dental hygiene.

Techno-Dent Training Center was located on Sixth Avenue between Thirty-First and Thirty-Second Street, and the majority of its students were recently arrived Russian immigrants. Reagan was really loosening things up with Gorbachev. The Russians were truly coming. It was rumored that Techno-Dent Training Center would receive larger sums of public money if they implemented an English as a Second Language program to supplement its core curriculum.

I've taught part-time ESL over the years but only when I have to. I respect ESL teachers. It requires a special kind of energy to be any good at it. A full-time ESL teacher, even certified or licensed, will probably do no more than eke out a living. There are those ESL teachers who teach ESL because it grants them the opportunity to teach all over the world, in places wherein they have a higher standard of living than in America and in places where they are accorded a much higher degree of respect. One such place is Asia, where I've heard that when a teacher enters a classroom, the students must stand—a far cry from the Land of the Free.

Most of my Russian students at Techno-Dent were in their sixties. None of them attended an institution of higher education. When I asked them about their jobs back in the USSR, I was given answers like barber, construction worker, mechanic, mother, grandmother, janitor, baker, gardener… And the one that stood out most was "I vork een zeh fectoree to make zeh meat." I was paid ten dollars per hour. This was a beginner class. I think I volunteered for this level, thinking it would be the most fun. I lasted through the new year and gave my notice the day after Techno-Dent's Christmas party, where buckets of Kentucky Fried Chicken were served, along with some warm watery rum punch.

Back at Brooklyn College, things went well. For the first time, I taught the rudiments of group discussion and broke down the class to groups of six so that each group could have their own group discussions in front of the rest of the class. About halfway through the semester, one of the full-time faculty members left a note in my mailbox requesting we set a date for an observation. The day arrived, and my observer failed to show. We arranged for another date. That day arrived, and again my observer failed to arrive. My would-be observer failed to get in touch with me after the second aborted observation. The semester was approaching the last quarter. I began thinking that I would not be observed after all.

Then one afternoon, while I was lecturing about group discussion, the door swung open. In came a gentleman with a bushel of gray hair atop his head. He walked with a slight stoop. He was dressed in his usual white shirt, tie, and gray slacks. This distinguished gentleman was none other than Dr. Charles Parkhurst, chairman of the Speech Department. Two things threw me—one, the element of total surprise; two, that my observer turned out to be the chairman of the department. You may recall that I was observed by Chairman Hesse at Kingsborough. But I didn't think of that observer as Chairman Hesse; I thought of him as Cliff. Cliff and I spoke and joked. Ours was quite the informal and relaxed professional relationship. But it was not so with Dr. Parkhurst.

While Dr. Parkhurst observed me, I remembered the expansive gesture I made while saying, "When you're in a group discussion with a problem to solve, it's important to let someone else exhaust his or her feelings and thoughts before responding. Premature interruption can stunt problem-solving."

Not only was my observation favorable, but Dr. Parkhurst mentioned that he would like me around "all the time in the future to teach speech."

On a cold midwinter's afternoon between the fall semester of '91 and the spring semester of '92, I nursed a glass of red wine in the Corner Bistro on the corner of West Fourth Street and Jane Street in Greenwich Village. The Bistro was a throwback to the days of Greenwich Village when you could meet writers and artists, when you could walk into any old and crummy bar and strike up conversations with strangers and perhaps discuss literature.

That afternoon, as I sat at the table closest to the door, I looked to my left. Two tables down, I recognized a figure I had seen many times in documentaries, a figure whose work I had read. It was Beat poet Gregory Corso. He was sitting with two other men. I went over and introduced myself, stating how much I liked his poetry and the fact that the Beats inspired me to begin writing my own poetry. He was flattered. He asked me to sit down.

"Oh, thank you very much. That would be such a pleasure. Just let me go back to my table and grab my book and drink."

"Get it," Gregory said.

And as I write these words and recall that two-word sentence that Gregory uttered, my spirits are lifted. At that point in my life, this was the type of person I wanted to meet—a poet. I'd been writing poetry for a good four years. I had read many biographies of poets, including Enid Starkie's studies of Baudelaire and Rimbaud, and devoured a biography of Allen Ginsberg a few years earlier. Prior to meeting Gregory, I had met Allen Ginsberg three times—once at Rapp Arts Center while I was rehearsing *Edward II*, once at a memorial for Abbie Hoffman, and once at one of Allen's performances in the East Village.

I returned to Gregory's table with my book and glass of red wine. I listened more than I spoke. The topics of conversation were not literary. That was fine with me. Anything that Gregory said was interesting to me. I had come to have a much greater respect for poets and writers in general than for actors. And by then, I knew how underappreciated poetry had become in the United States.

Over the next few months, I occasionally saw Gregory over a few drinks. He lived in the neighborhood, on Horatio Street, with a married couple. He wasn't working, and I didn't think he was writing either. In March, Gregory invited me to his sixty-second birthday party, which was held at the apartment of one of the men with whom he sat when I first met him. There I met Herbert Huncke and Allen Ginsberg's long-time lover, Peter Orlovsky. It was an interesting experience meeting and talking to people I had seen in documentaries or whose writings I had read.

During spring break of '92, I took my first trip to Europe—on my parents' dime. I travelled to London. When I disembarked at Heathrow, it was around seven in the morning. After going through the usual customs, I was asked to follow a woman. She led me down a staircase to a small low-ceilinged, fluorescent-lit room. A stern-looking man was waiting at the door. I was asked to sit down at a table. The woman who escorted me to the room sat across from me at the table along with the stern-looking man. She had a notebook in front of her and recorded my answers to the stern-looking man's questions.

"Is this your first trip to the continent?"

"Why did you choose London as your first city to visit in Europe?"

"Do you know anyone in the United Kingdom?"

"What do you plan on doing while here on holiday?"

"What is your occupation back in the States?"

"Do you have many friends back home?"

"Do you read books? What kind of books do you read?"

"Are you a member of any civic or political organizations?"

"Are you married?"

"Have you ever been married?"

What were the reasons for my detainment and interrogation? I was sober, wearing a tailored gray suit, and sporting a parted layered haircut. And I had been told for years that at certain angles, I looked English. So why the suspicion of this well-dressed, educated young man who could pass for a public relations man for the Anglican Church? Could I have been dressed like an IRA operative? Or was there simply a high alert on for lone well-dressed male travelers visiting London for the first time?

At one point during the interrogation, I asked if it would be all right if I smoked.

"I don't care if you burn," the stern-looking man replied.

After around forty minutes, the stern-looking man excused himself.

The woman sitting before me said, "He'll be right back."

When the stern-looking man returned, he sat down, looked at the woman, nodded his head, turned to me, and said, "Right. That'll be all, sir. Sorry to have kept you. I'll bring you back upstairs. Do you know where the taxi stand is?"

I sometimes think that this initial encounter with the English is the reason for my disinclination to read any of the Bronte sisters, Jane Austin, or Thomas Hardy.

But I had a splendid time in London. I stayed at the Hotel Rembrandt in Knightsbridge. I ate well, patronizing some fine restaurants, and I saw Albert Finney in a play in the West End. One morning, I virtually had the entire Otto Dix exhibit at the Tate Gallery to myself. This was my introduction to Expressionism. And what a way to experience it! I would share this incident with my students every time I began a lecture about Expressionism. When I went on a pub crawl in the East End, I felt like I was in a Dickens novel, what with those wonderful bar flies and their delicious cockney dialects. They were characters in the truest sense of the word. Funny lot—the English. Polite but cool. Open to a degree but always on their guard at bottom. Or so they seemed to me on my first visit.

I felt quite let down on my return to America. I wanted to return to London to live for a while. It seemed so romantic. Or perhaps the change of scenery and its culture overpowered me. Perhaps I simply needed some time outside of the US, and London seemed a safe bet. I'd been working hard, much harder than in my days as a struggling actor. An adjunct could never take reappointment for granted. I was never absent or late to my classes. Maybe my parents felt that I deserved a summer of romantic idling in Europe. They agreed to finance me. They knew I'd live modestly and responsibly. They trusted me as well.

A few weeks after arriving, I tried to find work, but it seemed an impossibility. On the summer of '92 in London, a great many nationals were out of work and on the dole. It was an economically depressed time for the UK. I mostly read books and newspapers and wrote poetry. I attended poetry readings and read some of my own poetry at a weekly reading held in a pub's basement. The poets were all men. The only bird was a girlfriend of a gentleman who simply came to listen to the poets. I found a small room with a private bath at the Hotel Edward, which still stands near Paddington Station in London Proper.

During my last week, I finally secured an interview to teach ESL at a school in Hammersmith run by a Turk. He was a nice man. He didn't even ask me for a sample lesson. He said he could use me. He offered me eight pounds an hour. He was unsure of how many hours per week, and there was a heap of red tape in order to obtain working papers, so I said no. The dream of London and its bridge had faded. I wouldn't risk sudden deportation, and the Turk's wages were quite low. And you recall how I feel about teaching ESL.

I arrived at John F. Kennedy International Airport sometime during the last week of August. My father greeted me at the airport. When he saw me emerge from the gate, his smile lit up the terminal. I'm sure he was happy to see me and happy to see me safe and sound.

On the fall of '92, I returned to my usual routine—one course at LIU, two courses at KCC, and a section of Voice and Diction at Brooklyn College. This course was devised to reduce both accents and dialects. I used the International Phonetic Alphabet as a reference, which I already knew from teaching Remedial English at KCC. By now I'd started writing a good deal of poetry. I bought the lie the Beats sold—that anyone could become a poet—for better or worse. It turned out to be an apprenticeship to other forms.

In September '92, after celebrating my birthday at a French bistro with my family, my mother and I discussed graduate school. At CUNY, an adjunct had to have earned at least a BA. I got the job at LIU through a connection. I knew I had to earn a master's to stay in the game and broaden my prospects. I would start graduate school in a year. Until then, I would continue my self-education and scribbling doggerel.

If an orthodox Jewish woman was alone in a public space with a man to whom she was not married, the door must be open. This was brought to my attention by one of my female students at Brooklyn College in the fall of '92. She approached me after class and asked to speak to me about a private matter.

"All right. Let me close the door."

"You can't do that," she said.

I complied and asked her what she wanted to talk about. She looked on the brink of tears.

"We don't have to do this right now," I said. "If you want to think it over some more before telling me, that's fine. You know where to find me."

"I think that's a good idea."

A week later, she approached me after class.

"You want to talk to me?"

"Yes."

"Let's go to my office."

It was around six. The secretary had left for the day. No one was in the Speech Department. I escorted her into an office belonging to a full-time professor who granted me the privilege of using it when he wasn't there.

"Don't close the door," she said.

I sat behind the desk.

"You have my full attention," I said.

"I'm pregnant." Then she started to cry.

Why was she telling me this? Did I project a presence of holy benevolence and supreme understanding? Or did this young woman grow up in an environment with a strict moral code and could find no one to lend an empathic ear?

I stood up and said, "I'm closing the door."

She nodded and wiped her eyes. It was one thing to advise a young man on where to go to help his father escape the clutches of alcoholism. This was something new altogether. This was not my business, and I had no right to make it my business. Maybe an ortho-dox Jewish female faculty member could make it her business but not me. This was foreign territory. Not only was this young woman a vir-tual stranger, but I had little knowledge of the sexual restrictions for unmarried women in the orthodox Jewish culture. Was it considered a sin to sleep with someone other than your husband? Was it a sin for a woman to share her bed with a man before marriage? I didn't like the position that I was suddenly put in. I had to play it very close to the vest. I sat down. Now she regained her composure.

"I take it you're not married to the young man?"

"He's my boyfriend."

"Who else knows?" I asked.

"No one."

"But you needed someone to tell."

She nodded her head.

That was all she really needed to do. She had no intention of actively seeking out my advice or counsel, smart young woman that she was. I told her that it was a complicated situation but that her next move was simple. She had to tell someone else. She couldn't carry this burden alone any longer, bad pun intended. I told her that if she were too scared to tell family and friends, there were social agencies she could go to—social agencies with hotlines that would not ask her for her personal information but would simply give her options. I told her that I couldn't get any more involved.

"I'm afraid we have to conclude this meeting now," I said.

The semester progressed. The young woman continued the class, and she never approached me again. By mid-December, I couldn't tell if she was showing because she was a rather heavy-set woman to begin with. When I administered the final exam, she was the very first student to finish. She placed her blue book and exam on my desk.

"Thank you," she said.

I never saw her again.

Spring 1993 delivered a few small but memorable victories. I was appointed to teach a Mass Media / Mass Communication course at KCC. This was way before the Internet and social media, so I was able to concentrate on print and broadcasting. And that was fine for the students. If you taught the same course today, I believe that the instructor would need to begin the semester by discussing social media.

Out of the many courses I have taught, this is one of my favorites. I'm the first to admit that television raised me. You don't have to be a media scholar to understand the profound impact that television had on the forming of minds for a certain segment of the baby boomers. This dubious honor, coupled with my love for film and magazines, allowed me a personal investment in my approach. I have taught the Mass Media / Mass Communication course a few times since, using the work of Daniel Boorstin and Neil Postman to deepen my understanding.

I discussed the genre of the men's magazine and the topic of discussion fell on *Esquire*. Then the name of Hugh Heffner came up, as well as how he played such an instrumental role in building the magazine's circulation. Then I turned to another kind of men's magazine—*Playboy*—and how Hugh Heffner branched out from *Esquire* to create this not-so-original brainchild. "Nudie" magazines had been around for many years, but these circulated through an underground market. You had to know the "right" people. And if you were found in possession of one, you might face a morals charge. But with *Playboy*, all you needed to do was walk up to a newsstand, reach for some change in your pocket, hand it over to the vendor, straighten your tie, and head back to your office.

Playboy was much more than a nudie magazine, and Hugh Heffner was much more than a flesh peddler. And there were other features to *Playboy*—short fiction, political commentary, pictorial lay-outs of the newest fashion for the successful male, and adult humor. It reached millions of readers through mainstream channels of commerce that were aboveboard. One of the term papers I received at the end of the semester was written by a young Black woman. It explored the empire of *Playboy* magazine. On the paper's cover page was the following title: "Hugh Heffner: Not just a flesh peddler." Small but memorable victory, this.

Another small victory at KCC was introducing a couple of students to two of the books that I loved. One of the students was a jittery yet lithe Hispanic with a pencil-thin mustache. There was a restlessness in him that I recognized on the very first day of class. To this young man, I introduced *Time of the Assassins* by Henry Miller. This is Henry Miller's tribute to French poet Arthur Rimbaud. You can appreciate it on more than one level, not the least of which is ecstatic appreciation one writer has for another. Another level is Miller's dissection of the poet's role in society. Another is Miller's facile psychological analysis of Rimbaud. And, too, there is the sheer buoyancy of Miller's prose. There are enough goodies on the plate to choose from.

When I handed the young man the book, he immediately turned to the first page and began reading.

"Thank you," he said, "but why me?"

"Why *not* you?" I rejoined.

Another student to whom I introduced one of my more exciting and informative reads was a rotund young man with a jolly disposition. If he'd been dressed in red velvet and had a white beard on him and a red stocking cap on his head, he could have easily played Santa Claus's young understudy. Why would I give a copy of Jean Paul Sartre's *Anti-Semite and Jew* to such a young man? Like *Time of the Assassins*, you can appreciate *Anti-Semite and Jew* on more than one level, not the least of which is its probing examination of the bigoted and racist mind. In the spring of '92, news of the Brooklyn killing of Yusef Hawkins and the Crown Heights riot were still fresh. Racism in America would always be a fresh topic of discussion, even if dishonestly approached. I was sure this young man could take something away from Sartre's work. *Anti-Semite and Jew* was terrifically accessible.

Both young men thanked me when they returned the books, and both told me they enjoyed it—small but sweet victories.

In spring of '92, two of my poems appeared in *Downtown Brooklyn: A Journal of Writing*, which was published through LIU's English Department. One of my poems, "The Once Bashful Motor-Man," is a rather abstruse piece of doggerel about masturbation. The other poem is about my maternal grandmother.

Gristle & Mercy

shades of Sylvia
mother of my mother
you
are
lost to the laughter and
facility of
blurred gatherings,
celebrations and
callow chats,

"Mazel Tovs" & plentiful spreads,
abominable Mitzvah bands,
in a hollow circle our tribe held hands,
jewELRY/GERMan cars and lettuce leaves,
of these paltry joys shroud in favor of the
chosen
two

a
drizzling afternoon
I'm four
You & I
seated at a fluorescent lit luncheonette on
Kings Highway,
I taste a piece of gristle
In the flesh of my patty,

I grimaced and spit out my mouthful
to the chuckle of the
pock-marked counterman,
you then
reached for the bun
with wrinkled hands
topped by ruby-red nails
and bit down &
by the shake of your head and arched brows
you told me
the burger's not bad

didn't you notice the gristle?
or care?
or
maybe you kept notice and care hidden
so you'd be the source of my nourishment
for just a moment?

and what's a piece of gristle compared to
running from pogrom?

years later
on a night
in the wake of
yuletide cheer
your frail frame
carried out of your
daughter's home
by your son
his laced hands
wrapped 'round your belly
as a little boy carries
his mother's new china
in a paper box,
this to your protest
fueled by anguished concession,
tired of buying
some
more
time
at Mt. Sinai's ICU
for your failing heart

I don't know
how much time elapsed
when your daughter said to me,
"it was His blessing."

PART III

PARIS AND BEYOND

As spring semester '93 came to an end, Cliff called me up and offered me a summer class in Remedial English. I eagerly accepted.

I had recently come into a small inheritance left me by an aunt. It was not a great sum but was enough for me to see Europe. I chose Paris. When I told Gregory Corso I'd be going at the end of the summer, he said, "You'll love it. Give me a piece of paper." I tore a sheet from my notebook. Gregory pulled a pen from his shirt pocket and wrote the following: "Geo, a friend of ours." Then he signed his name, and under that, he wrote an excellent facsimile of Allen Ginsberg's signature.

"There's an American language bookstore called Shakespeare and Company. Rue de la Bucherie. Show this paper to the owner. His name is George."

"Okay." I asked no questions.

On my flight to Paris, shortly after takeoff, a comely priest walked down my aisle and offered the passengers his blessings. I slipped through customs at Charles de Gaulle Airport as easily as I slipped through my mother's womb. I checked into Les Argonautes at 12 Rue de la Huchette after the most enjoyable cab ride of my life. Les Argonautes was a modest but comfortable hotel situated in the 5th Arrondissement. I took a short nap. Then I showered, dressed, and descended the swirling staircase three flights down to the lobby, ready for my first evening in the City of Light. I asked the concierge for directions to Rue de la Bucherie.

"You a fast walker, monsieur?"

"Tres," I said.

"Chic alors. Then you can be there in one minute."

"Merci beaucoup."

"De rien."

It was about six in the evening, a stubborn sunlight holding fast to the oncoming dusk. Shakespeare and Company sat across from Notre Dame. On Sunday mornings, you could hear its clanging bells.

I walked in. A young man sat behind a desk, reading a Grove Press edition of Henry Miller's *Tropic of Cancer*.

"Bon soir," I said.

"Can I help you?" He was an American.

"I'm looking for Geo."

"Who?"

"Geo, the owner of the store."

"Oh, that would be George. He's upstairs, cooking."

I passed him the piece of paper that Gregory signed.

"Uh-huh," he said as he passed back the piece of paper. "You go straight back to the end of the first floor, go up the stairs to the second floor, then to the rear, past the rare book section, and you'll see him."

"Thank you."

When I reached the second floor, I smelled onions. I reached a room where I saw a man in front of a range. There was a pot of boiling onions, a pot of boiling peeled potatoes, and a pot of boiling carrots. The old man standing in front of the range kept watch over the onions while stirring the carrots.

"Good evening," I said.

"Yeah?"

"Are you George?"

"Who are you?"

I handed him the piece of paper.

A moment passed. Then he chuckled. He asked, "Need a bed?"

If you were an intelligent woman who happened upon Shakespeare and Company and seemed like a vagrant or simply in need of a roof over your head and if you caught George in the right mood, he'd extend an invitation and even offer a hot meal right then and there. Men were a different story. Men needed a letter of introduction, which was exactly what Gregory gave me. Dear Gregory probably knew what George's reaction would be when I showed him the letter.

The idea of staying at a bookstore in Paris, right across the street from Notre Dame, had never occurred to me. And I was right in not asking Gregory what the letter meant or what it would bring. I was shocked. This was the first time in my life that a stranger offered me "a bed." But it was my first time in Paris, and I already checked into my hotel. I chickened out. I promptly thanked George, informing him that I had already checked into Les Argonautes and that I reserved the room for six days.

"Well," he said, "a little later, we're having a cocktail party of sorts and a poetry reading in front of the store. You're welcome to come if you like."

Folding chairs were placed in front of the store. I was in Paris at a poetry reading at an internationally renowned bookstore. I had taught myself some French. I had a glass of wine in my hand. George would make the rounds of the gathered crowd, passing out chunks of brie. It was a comfortable late August evening, breezy and mild. I was sitting amid refined and lettered people. The poet was announced. His poems celebrated life and language, and he recited with a heart full of joy. He talked about sestinas. I said hello to him after the reading, and he thanked me for attending. Now the moon was full. This was the closest I had ever come to nirvana.

Before I returned to New York, George informed me, "You're welcome here anytime." He kept his word, to the letter.

In the fall of '93, I entered the MA program in theatre at Hunter College—CUNY. This was a program grounded in scholarship and research, not performance. I was ready for the rigors of scholarship. I had little to none of it as an undergraduate. When I graduated from Boston University, I had, as John Houseman refers to the minds of his first-year law students in the film *The Paper Chase*, "a skull full of mush."

To earn an MA in Theatre at Hunter, you had to earn thirty-two credits and write a thesis. And you had to maintain at least a B average. I started at Hunter on nonmatriculated status. You could earn up to nine credits and then transfer them if you chose to matriculate. I registered for two three-credit courses. One class was Theatre History I, which was taught by Vera Roberts, who, legend had it, was one of the original founders of the Arena Stage in Washington, DC. My other class was a seminar on The Group Theatre, which was taught by Hellen Krich Chinoy, a visiting professor from Middlebury College in Vermont. I received a B in Theatre History and a B– in The Group Theatre seminar. It was not a very auspicious start, but it was only opening night.

When Cliff Hesse asked me if I was interested in teaching business communication for the Business Department for spring '94, I felt like responding as Grouch Marx did when offered an opportunity to host a TV quiz show: "Sir, do you live in a tree?" What did I know of the world of business? The extent of my business acumen stopped at recognizing the difference between merchant and consumer. I had never occupied a corporate position. I had never taken a business course. I had never taken an economics course. I had never read the Business Section in *The New York Times*. I didn't understand the stock market. I thought only aspiring models had portfolios. I didn't understand what a bond was. I didn't know the difference between a hedge fund and a slush fund. I didn't understand what determined interest rates.

I couldn't remember having a conversation with a businessman about how businesses were run or what the priorities of a businessman were. I was surely not a company man. I knew that I could never learn the rules of the games corporate people played with one another and with their competition. Corporate settings unnerved me. It made me nervous to see someone sitting behind a desk whose primary responsibility was to "receive" me like I was a letter slipped through a slot. I never took to corporate culture nor its structure. It seemed a *Junior Miss* version of the armed forces. Nine to five, one hour for lunch, two weeks a year for vacation. A company Christmas party. Words like *secretary, account executive, junior manager of billing and sales, payroll manager*... How could I possibly teach a course that was so alien to my sensibility and understanding?

"Are you sure I'd be suited to teach business communication?" I asked.

Business Communication was a different kind of course than I thought. It was a course targeted to undergraduate liberal arts majors on how to market themselves when trying to enter the labor force. The course also instructed students on how to conduct themselves both verbally and nonverbally within a business context. Cliff said I could spend at least two to three weeks strengthening the students' employment interview skills. This I could do. Cliff said that they needed a lot of help in constructing marketable résumés and well-written cover letters. This I could do. And there should be an oral component to the course. Students would be required to make a five-minute informative speech about a topic connected with either the world of business or business communication.

"You mean a student could do a speech describing the process of how Nathan's Famous was launched?" I asked.

"Absolutely."

"Or a speech describing the different materials for procurement and how much they would cost when a corporation built an amusement park?"

"That's good too."

"Or how about a speech describing white-collar crime?"

I met with the chairman of the Business Department, and he told me that Cliff was correct in his description of the course content and expectations of students and that the instructor did not have to have a "head for business." But it would help if I occasionally glanced at *The New York Times*'s Business Section or even the *New York Post*'s Business Page just to give myself a bit of grounding in the goings-on in the business world. It would also grant me more credibility with the students. During the interim between the fall of '93 and spring of '94 semesters, I strolled down to the Jefferson Market branch of the New York Public Library and did a little research on Nathan's Famous, the frankfurter empire. I figured it would be an interesting business model to talk about. Here was a real example of a mom-and-pop business literally starting on the street on the corner of Surf and Coney Island Avenues and then mushrooming to the most successful level of retail incorporation.

And what better way to begin a semester than by asking the class, "How many people here like hot dogs?"

I began the spring of '94 with two courses at KCC—Business Communication and the Golden Age of Radio. Added to these were two courses of Oral Communications, one at Brooklyn College and one at Long Island University. I returned to Hunter College as a matriculated graduate student in its MA Theatre program. I enrolled in one course, which was taught by noted film and theatre critic Stanley Kauffmann, whose film reviews I'd been reading for years in *The New Republic*. The course was called the History of Directors. It was a survey course of twelve major figures from theatre history who had been instrumental in developing the figure and function of the stage director. One of these figures turned out to be Antonin Artaud, the French poet, actor, theatre director, essayist, surrealist, and sketch artist.

I first became familiar with Antonin Artaud when I acted in *Artaud at Rodez*, a play that explores Artaud's stay at the titular psychiatric hospital and his relationship with his doctor, Gaston Ferdiere. The play was performed at Boston University in the fall of my senior year. It was performed in a dance studio. I played Charles Dullin, one of Artaud's stage directors. *Artaud at Rodez* was directed by my movement teacher, Bob Finlay. To give the cast a deeper understanding of the work and mind of Antonin Artaud, Bob had us read a collection of Artaud's essays, *The Theatre and Its Double*, one of the most widely read twentieth-century books on theatre. In it, Artaud advances his theory on what the experience of theatre should be for the spectator, which he describes as a "Theatre of Cruelty."

I was twenty-one years old the first time I read *The Theatre and Its Double*—too young and inexperienced to understand the ideas. But when I read it again some eleven years later as a graduate student—as a man who had experienced his fair share of disappointment, rejection, joy, frustration, and a good year's worth of consistent headache spells unrelieved by either doctors or medicine—my reaction was altogether different. I had some deeply felt reads before, but not since Henry Miller's *Sexus* had prose so naturally altered my brain chemistry. I loved the way Artaud's mind worked. I loved his unpredictability and the utter indifference to his reader's reaction to his radical ideas of what theatre, literature, film, and the plastic arts could be. I loved his writing style. As Charles Bukowski said when speaking of John Fante's work, "It came from the gut."

And I could so sympathize with his physical ailments, of which there were many throughout his short life. Some people thought him mad, given his erratic behavior and his involuntary admittance to Rodez. He had a lifelong laudanum habit, more to ease his physical pain than for manufactured sensations. I had more than a mere affinity for the man and his work. When reading him, I felt possession; the possession then changed to obsession after putting the book down. For the first time in my life, I felt I found a genuine kindred spirit, and his spirit haunted me. Artaud died in 1948. His spirit would emerge again, forty-eight years later, in the body of this memoir's author. I decided to write a play about him with the full intention of portraying him. My appreciation for poet Antonin Artaud echoed the ecstatic appreciation that Henry Miller had for poet Arthur Rimbaud.

As the spring semester of '94 came to an end, so began my journey into the chaotic but brilliant mind of Antonin Artaud. From June of '94 until December '95, I would read all that I could about Artaud. I also read a good deal about the Surrealist movement. I continued teaching, but the play became my primary focus. I worked with a frenzy, taking prodigious handwritten notes along the way. At the end of the summer of '94, I returned to my beloved Paris.

This time, when George Whitman offered me a bed, I accepted. The first night, I slept on the second floor. What George called a bed was not really a bed at all. It was more like long wooden seating that accommodated a body. Line the wood with a blanket and put one over you, and you have your "bed." Several people slept on these wooden beds, and some people slept on the floor. When I woke the following morning and helped open the shop, as guests were required to do, George informed me that I could move into the Antiquarian Room for the rest of my stay.

"I'm making you writer in residence," George said as he took a key from his key ring and opened the Antiquarian Room's wooden door.

I got the feeling that, as payback for free lodging, George wanted me to hang around the store and greet the customers and give them some assistance if they needed it. The Antiquarian Room was around thirteen by thirteen in diameter. Its entrance was street level, around seven feet from the main shop's entrance. The walls were lined with ceiling-high bookshelves. On the shelves were the rarest of editions, covering a wide range of subjects and genres. The first book I looked at was a thin Gardner's manual by an Irish botanist, published in 1912. There was a standard twin mattress atop a rickety iron fame. A raggedy gray blanket lay over the rock-hard mattress.

George gave me a key of my own. The store closed at eleven. After that, I was free to come and go as I pleased, just so long as I locked the door. When you resided in the main shop, you had to be back at the shop at closing time to secure your bed space. I wondered what I had done to gain George's trust. I had to be careful not to drink too much if I chose to go out late, lest I lost my key. There was no toilet either. I managed to improvise my way through this inconvenience. If I wanted to shower, there were the public baths dispersed throughout the city. There was a single light switch that, when turned on, illuminated the room with a harsh fluorescent light. I asked George if I could light a couple of candles after closing time.

"You plumb loco? I got some of the rarest editions in the world in this room."

For the next seven days, I mostly hung around the store and worked on my play *Artaud for Awhile*. I also wrote a celebrative piece on Shakespeare and Company, in pencil, which George read and liked. When I spent time in the Antiquarian Room during business hours, I could meet people from all over the world and sometimes discuss literature. I felt more at home there than I did in Manhattan. On a Sunday morning in the wee hours, as I lay on my bed, not a soul to be heard from outside the door, I had a strange thought. Lying there in the pitch-black darkness, surrounded by cloth and leather-bound rare editions, I imagined myself a convict in a progressive penologist's new model for solitary confinement, my crime having been grand-scale book piracy. A few hours later, I was pleasantly awakened by the clanging bells of Notre Dame.

I enrolled at Hunter for the fall semester of '94, had my usual course load from CUNY and LIU, and continued my research for *Artaud for Awhile*. I was never so obsessed. I still enjoyed teaching, but *Artaud for Awhile* became my priority. This was truly a labor of love. I finished a first draft a few hours before accompanying my father to a performance of *Inherit the Wind* on Broadway, featuring George C. Scott as Drummond.

The first forty minutes of *Artaud for Awhile* consists of Artaud talking to the audience. Based on my research, it details his life with its problems, hardships, frustrations, and occasional triumph. At times, he's irreverent to his audience but always in a spirit of play. After Artaud completes his monologue to the audience, Jim Morrison enters. I knew that Jim Morrison was a reader of Artaud from seeing the Oliver Stone film *The Doors*. Jim Morrison makes his presence in the play in order to bring Artaud through a sexual encounter. The monologue worked, whereas the scene between Artaud and Morrison, though clever in uniting two icons who are at once quite similar and quite different, did not. It was more gimmick than dramatic action and conflict.

In April of '96, I enrolled in another class taught by Stanley Kauffmann at Hunter. Sometime earlier, I read Stanley's review of *En compagnie d'Antonin Artaud* in *The New Republic*. The film had its original release in Paris in 1993. Stanley gave the film a tepidly favorable review, but I knew he liked Artaud and thought his work important. The film was given a limited screening in New York and with very little advertising. I think it ran for a week or so. I liked Stanley, and he seemed to like me. After class one night, I asked him if he would be kind enough to read a copy of *Artaud for Awhile*. He agreed. After the conclusion of the following week's class, he asked to see me. He told me that he hadn't had a chance to read the play yet but that he would try his best to read it by the following class.

"There's no hurry," I said. "Whenever you get the chance is fine. I know you're a busy man."

After the following class, he asked to see me again. "Let's go to my office," he said.

His feedback was positive and encouraging. Whatever his true feelings on the play, I believe he championed and admired the effort involved. Stanley respected the creative urge and the completion of the creative product, for in addition to being a renowned critic, he had also written several novels. Though he was not recognized as a novelist, his position in American letters was secure. With that strong sense of self and his accomplishments outside of academia, he would respect and encourage the creative efforts of a young man.

When *Artaud for Awhile* was completed, I needed a space to flesh it out.

At Hunter College, I met an older graduate student named Duane Mazey in Stanley's History of Directors class. Duane and I spoke sometimes before class started. He had a theatre background. He mentioned some technical experience but little else regarding performing or directing. When Hunter started up again in the fall of '96, I called Duane and told him about the play and if he knew of any companies in New York that might be interested in producing it. He said he'd like to read it first. He read it, liked it, and told me he knew of a space where it could be performed. Duane knew a Jeff Corrick, the artistic director of Wings Theatre, a nonprofit off-off Broadway company in the Archive Building at 154 Christopher Street in Manhattan. Duane wanted to direct it as well. I said, "Of course."

So around the second week of September, Duane, Jeff Corrick, and I met at the Wings Theatre in the production office. It was arranged that *Artaud for Awhile* would play on Tuesday and Wednesday nights for three weeks, beginning November 20th. I would charge $12 per ticket. The house would keep 60 percent of the box office receipts, and I would keep the rest. I would not be charged a fee for the nights of performance, and Wings would grant me the use of the performance space for rehearsals on weekday mornings based on availability. What an unheard-of anomaly in the annals of unknown and beginning playwrights! My very first play was given a fully staged production without me submitting a query to theaters, much less submitting the first ten pages of dialogue or the entire manuscript and then waiting for six months to a year for a reply. My very first play found a home in a seventy-five seat house with a proscenium arch in the heart of Greenwich Village. And with all this, I was being given the opportunity to earn some money! Ye gods!

And speaking of gods, when the fall semester of '96 began, I began teaching at the Men's division of Yeshiva University in Washington Heights in Manhattan. I came to this position after being referred by Dr. Richard Helfer, a fellow adjunct at KCC. The students were orthodox. They were also my most literate, well-educated, and disciplined students. I was to teach, yet again, the course Speech Communications. I taught two sections two days a week. The wage stank, but it was higher than LIU and a pleasant place to teach. During the fall of '96, I was spreading myself around like chicken fat on soda crackers. I was teaching two courses at Yeshiva University in Upper Manhattan for the very first time, one course at Long Island University in downtown Brooklyn, and two courses at Kingsborough Community College in Manhattan Beach, Brooklyn. One of the courses I taught at KCC was new for me, Freshman Writing, which I bungled terribly. I was taking a demanding graduate course at Hunter, and most importantly, I had a demanding lead role in a play that I wrote. As John Lydon proclaims in Public Image Limited, "Anger is an energy."

Duane and I met at Wings Theatre on a Saturday to hold open-call auditions. I expected to audition many actors because both parts called for attractive performers in their twenties and I had placed an ad in Backstage. The actors auditioning for the part of Jim Morrison read from the script. The actresses reading for the part of Raven St. Clair, the woman with whom Artaud has the off-stage but audible sexual encounter, interpreted a prose poem I wrote.

For the role of Jim Morrison, we cast a young actor named Jonathan. He gave an excellent performance. For the role of Raven, we cast a leggy redhead, who also turned in an excellent performance.

In the fall of '96 came a resurgence of interest in the life and work of Artaud. It was the centennial of Artaud's birth. Another actor was performing the role somewhere downtown. His picture appeared in a small notice in *The Village Voice*, announcing the play. There was also a well-publicized exhibit of Artaud's drawings at the Museum of Modern Art. He was suddenly in vogue. How would I capitalize on this and generate interest in the play that I spent nearly two years writing? I had money in the bank, but it was not nearly enough to hire a freelance publicist. I did the most I could with what I had.

My friend Nick's girlfriend, Margaret, studied at the School of Visual Arts in Manhattan. I showed her a photograph of Artaud as he appeared in the part of the young monk Jean Massieu in Carl Dryer's 1928 silent film, *The Passion of Joan of Arc*. Artaud is photographed from a low angle. Artaud is strikingly handsome here, his eyes focused above the camera's lens. I gave Margaret some ideas of how to design the flyer based on the photograph. What I asked her to do was to reproduce the original photograph in drawing, with one qualification. I asked her to see if she could render Artaud's features a bit like mine. Cowering behind Artaud, in much smaller dimensions but his darkly handsome presence just as pronounced, would be a shirtless Jim Morrison. I was very happy with Margaret's work. I paid her 150 dollars. I paid another 150 dollars for a 3 × 3.5 inch ad in *The Village Voice*. The ad was basically a copy of the flyer, with the dates and times of the performances, the price of tickets, and the box office phone number. I think the ad ran for an entire week, as *The Village Voice* was a weekly.

But the most unexpected and, as it turned out, free bit of publicity came in a thirty-second sound bite on 99.5 WBAI, one of New York City's independent radio stations. I mailed one of the in-house hosts, a Janet Coleman, a press release of the play. I got her on the phone at WBAI. A few days later, in the wee morning hours—say, around one—about three weeks into rehearsal and about a week and a half from opening night, my project was announced on the radio.

It didn't cost me one red penny. As an independent and nonprofit station, WBAI was commercial free. It could be that Janet was doing a favor for someone. Or maybe she liked the premise of the play or fancied either Artaud or Jim Morrison or both. Things like this were more likely to occur in 1996, when people were more likely to kowtow to their whimsy and cared less for rules and regulations. People were more generous and unpredictable, more in the moment.

One Saturday afternoon, I visited the Artaud exhibit at the Museum of Modern Art. The exhibit mainly consisted of his drawings, most of which he created while hospitalized during the last few years of his life. There were also some of his original letters and poems. These were encased in glass. I managed to place a stack of flyers on a couple of these glass encasements, undetected by museum security. I'm not sure if anyone attended a performance of *Artaud for Awhile* as a result of seeing flyers or any other of my modest promotional efforts, but the house on opening night was at least three-quarters capacity. For the eight o'clock curtain, we opened the house at seven thirty. At about seven forty, I walked through a corridor that led to the back-of-house lighting-and-sound booth. I was certainly surprised. I recognized a few students from Long Island University, no one else.

The opening night's performance went well enough. I sensed audience appreciation and involvement. I wasn't sure of Artaud's appeal for the audience, but for the forty-eight minutes that I spoke to the audience, I didn't hear any coughing nor sighs, nor could I detect anyone becoming restless in their seats. In hindsight, I believe the audience witnessed an actor celebrating what he thought to be the character's self-dramatization. I pulled no punches in presenting who and what the man was. It was a faithful and traditional rendition. About halfway into the run, there was the one and only sold-out house. Better one than none, especially since this was off-off Broadway.

Sometime during the third and last week of performances, the management at Wings Theatre offered to extend the run. I was offered an additional two weeks beginning the third week of January.

During the interim, I made some revisions that merely changed rather than helped the narrative. I sent out a press release to many local magazines and newspapers, hoping for a reviewer to attend a performance, but to no avail. For the extended two-week run, most of the houses were small but appreciative and attentive. What little money I made from the project I partied away, treating my small cast and crew to food and drink after several performances.

When the extended run concluded, little in my life seemed different. I occupied the same teaching posts at the same schools, earned the same income, and continued to live from paycheck to paycheck. I failed to forge any valuable theatre contacts as an actor or a playwright. I moved in the same limited professional and social circles. *The Village Voice* had listed the play as one of its *Voice*'s picks. How and why this occurred remains a mystery. One thing is certain, though; the entire experience changed me. It was the first time I ever felt genuinely creative. This labor of love certainly brought forth a sweet-smelling fruit richer than the temporary fattening of my billfold.

One day I became impregnated with the mere seed of an original idea and eventually witnessed its birth. My child had a short lifetime, but his spirit lives on. I was thirty-five years old when *Artaud for Awhile* was produced. I had little money, few friends, no girlfriend, and no children. *Artuad for Awhile* was a dream come true within a dream come true. When I was a little boy, I dreamed of becoming an actor, and I did. Later, I dreamed of writing a play about the poet and aesthetician Antonin Artaud and portraying him on stage, and both became a reality. As Delmore Schwartz averred, "In dreams begin responsibilities."

During the winter and summer breaks in between semesters, many adjuncts are on the street, hustling for income. Sometimes an adjunct can have an open claim and certify for unemployment benefits. If an adjunct has a verbal offer from a college to return to work after the break, the Department of Labor might not come through with the weekly checks. After *Artaud for Awhile* closed in mid-January of '97, I was flat broke. When I saw an ad in *The New York Times* seeking a part-time reservationist for the three-star restaurant, the Blue Water Grill, in Union Square, I responded. It was a straight-salaried position. It was a respectable hourly wage. When interviewed, I mentioned to the manager that I taught speech communications at the college level.

"Okay, that's it," he concluded. "You're hired."

My responsibilities included taking reservations over the phone and answering questions about the menu or wine list. All reservations were taken by phone, then uploaded to a computer. The manager gave me two days of paid training to learn the system of uploading the reservations online. Industry was on its way to complete digitalization. I was still writing on a manual typewriter. I needed those two days of training.

I arrived for my first day of training at 11:00 a.m. sharp. I was trained by a stringy blonde. When I asked her how old she was, she said she was nineteen. When I answered a call, she shared the line. If the party requested a reservation, she guided me to upload it on the computer. I was slow to learn, but I was learning. My trainer was patient and easy to work with. The few times she hinted at a smile was while I talked to certain parties about the menu.

When asked about appetizers, I began with "Well, we have a lovely escargot," affecting the slightest of French accents.

When asked about the entrées, I replied, "We have a wide range of cuisine—from pastas to different cuts of steak to chicken and veal to fish. We make a wonderful hamburger. And we always have daily specials. Is there a particular dish that you're interested in?"

Sometimes the party cut me off and asked about the pastas or the veal. Sometimes the party cut me off and asked about the steaks. The only time I looked at the menu was when a party asked me about the prices. I felt I was presenting the restaurant in quite the positive light and generating reservations. When asked about the wine, I always began with French labels because I could effect a French accent.

At around three in the afternoon, after uploading reservations without any assistance, my trainer suggested that I get some lunch. "You can take an hour," she said.

I went to a pizzeria on Fourth Avenue for a couple of slices and returned to the restaurant. I took a half hour instead of an hour. When I returned, the manager who hired me was standing behind the hostess.

I said hello.

"Come with me," he said.

I followed him through a long and dimly lit corridor. He stopped at a door and opened it with a key.

He entered and said, "Come in."

He switched on a light. There was a lone desk and a chair behind it. On top of the desk, there sat a tin box.

"This isn't going to work out," he said.

"I don't—"

"You're not working quickly enough. I need someone to learn the system like this." He snapped his fingers three times in rapid succession.

"But I thought that's why you gave me the two days of training in which to—"

"I'm sorry, but you're out of your realm."

Then he unlocked the tin box, reached in, and extracted a bill. He walked over to me and put it in my hand. It was a fifty.

"You people…" I murmured.

"I'm sorry. C'mon. I'm very busy."

Then he stood outside the door in the corridor. I left the room. The last time he looked me in the eye was when I greeted him at the reception area. He locked the door. Then he turned to me and began to say something.

I stopped him in midsentence and said, "Well, I guess civility and literacy aren't needed in this business."

Then I turned and walked away. When I turned around to shoot him a final optic dagger, there he stood, frozen in dumb amazement, mouth agape, stripped clean of his arrogance.

Why bite when a growl will do just as well, if not better?

On a bright and early spring afternoon in the following April, I received a call from Earl Perkins, the director of the summer program at Cushing Academy. Earl was in the market for a master teacher in oral communications for the upcoming summer session. Cushing Academy is a coeducational, nonsectarian private high school in Ashburnham, Massachusetts. It's about forty miles from Boston proper. My younger brother received his high school diploma from Cushing Academy on a perfectly ideal spring morning in 1983. I remember offering him a congratulatory nod as he accepted an award for distinguished achievement in Cushing's drama society.

Sometime in the early '90s, I flew up to Cushing Academy in early winter. There was an opening for an English teacher for the following year's term, beginning in September and lasting through late June. The position offered a decent salary along with benefits and free room and board. The academic director interviewed me. Joe and I sat on high-backed leather chairs a good ten feet from each other. I was quite comfortable during the interview, not the nervous youngster I was when interviewed by Mortimer Becker. Words easily came this time. Within minutes, Joe sensed my love of literature, and we were at ease. The interview lasted for over an hour. I suppose I projected an identifiable idealism. I was still relatively new to teaching.

"I can tell you right away that you'll be given strong consideration," Joe said at the interview's end.

Joe phoned me a few weeks later. This time, our conversation was brief and pedestrian. He seemed embarrassed and in quite a hurry to end the conversation. It turned out that whoever filled the position of English teacher would need to double as varsity ice hockey coach. I had seen one amateur and two professional hockey games. I was not a fan.

"I guess I'm not your man," I said.

After Earl Perkins talked a little about the summer session's mission, he said, "I need a good oral communications teacher. The job's yours if you want it."

When I arrived at Cushing Academy in mid-June, I had been living in Manhattan for thirteen years. I was a city boy through and through. My biggest mistake was in not renewing my driver's license. When I went to the Department of Motor Vehicles in early May, I was informed that I had to take both the written and driving test again because my license expired three years earlier and too much time had passed.

What's the big deal? I thought. *It's only talking six weeks. I'll be fine.*

I grossly underestimated the adjustment. In addition to teaching three sections of oral communications that met Monday through Saturday mornings, I was hired to serve as house resident. I lived on the second floor in a prewar colonial. I had a small living room, a small bedroom, and for the first time in my adult life, a separate kitchen. As a house resident, I was responsible for being on the premises from 9:00 p.m. onward five nights a week. Six boys equally shared three bedrooms on the ground floor. Two boys were Turkish, two were Italian, and two were American. They were no trouble at all to look after.

By now, I was so familiar with the content of a basic oral communications course that I could sleep-walk my way through teaching one. And for the first two or so weeks of the summer session, that was just what I did—not by choice, but because I was having such trouble getting a good night's sleep. It was just too quiet outside my bedroom window. There I lay each night on the second floor of a house at the base of a hill in Ashburnham, Massachusetts. Beyond the campus, the town consisted of a modest shopping plaza and a gas station adjacent to a pizzeria that served slices I wouldn't give to a city rat I didn't like. I pined to hear any sound at all as I lay in bed. There were no crickets nor the rustling of leaves from a summer's breeze. Occasionally, I heard a human voice from a distance. Occasionally, I heard an automobile's running engine. How I wished to hear a fire engine, an ambulance, a patrol car's siren.

I walked into my first morning class after a night of stealing ten minutes of slumber here, twenty minutes there. I tried sleeping on the floor. I tried sleeping naked. I tried tiring myself out doing as many sets of pushups as possible without going into cardiac arrest. Those first couple of weeks, I really developed my deltoids and pectorals, but I still experienced sleep deprivation. In my studio apartment in Manhattan, my windows faced the street, approximately ten feet below. There were nights that I fell asleep to the bustling of semis, automobiles, speeding taxis, voices of every conceivable texture, drunks muttering to themselves, couples arguing, the schizophrenic homeless screaming at the illusionary voices talking to them and cackling at their hallucinations. I was homesick.

Falling asleep to absolute silence was just too great an adjustment for my nervous system. I tried drinking a glass of wine, which worsened the situation. The wine simply mudded my thoughts. During my evenings off, I took long walks. Still no help. The country air seemed to have an energizing effect. One afternoon, I was strolling around the biography section in Cushing's library. I thought of taking a book out that was a different kind of read for me. I chose *The Autobiography of Benjamin Franklin*. When he began reflecting on his family's ancestry, I started to fade. But when he started talking about his uncle Benjamin, my eyelids began to grow heavy. When he invoked his Uncle Ben's poetry, that was the clincher. I fell asleep and stayed asleep.

The next morning, I felt an odd sense of patriotism and a fondness for our founding fathers. And for the first time, I welcomed the chirping birds outside my window. Up until that morning, I always heard the birds chirping as a sort of mocking, as if they were ribbing me at my failure to adjust to country living. So each night after getting in bed, I picked up ole Ben's bio and let his clunky and long-winded prose lull me to sleep. I spent my mornings teaching my sections and then had lunch.

The highlight of my day turned out to be watching reruns of the seventies crime dramas *Cannon* and *The Rockford Files* on a local station. One afternoon, on an episode of *Cannon*, the lead actor, William Conrad, was investigating a small group of disenfranchised Vietnam veterans who were planning to hijack the receipts of a local stadium's accounting department. Cannon tried to thwart the hijacking by posing as an ex-police officer who was thrown off the force for corruption. Cannon was indeed an ex-police officer, but the part about being thrown off the force for corruption was a complete fabrication.

Taking on this fabricated identity, he walked into a bar where he knew the vets were gathered. He feigned drunkenness. He asked for a drink at the bar, and the bartender told him he'd had enough and turned his back on Cannon. Then Cannon went into a quiet tirade, chastising the bartender for his impertinence to an older and more experienced man. When Cannon completed his quiet tirade and secured a drink from the bartender, he made a grand gesture with the back of his hand and uttered in a beautifully affected manner, "Now you may go." I laughed so hard they could have heard me in Maine. I laughed so hard that my brain probably released enough endorphins to stave off any present or future virus waiting in the wings to weaken and cripple my unsuspecting immune system.

Over the next several days, students and faculty and staff members could see me walking around campus and suddenly breaking into a pronounced yet devilishly self-contained giggle. This was a result from a willed recall of the aforementioned episode of television's *Cannon*. It had been my observation that Cushing's environment took on what I thought was an unnecessarily somber tone. People seemed bound by an unwritten code of behavior. I was naïve enough to believe that a private academy in New England for teens could be anything less than corporate. Cushing Academy was certainly a professionally managed outfit, and I realized the task administration had in being responsible for the welfare of the students, most of whom lived on campus. Yet it was a fiercely prosaic environment rife with too many rules and regulations. You had to eat in the cafeteria at only certain times. Campus was completely tobacco free. I was banned from having a cigarette in the privacy of the house where I lived after the students had gone to bed.

The rules and regulations wouldn't have mattered as much had I found faculty and administration somewhat friendlier. Most, if not all, administrative staff and faculty members worked at Cushing during the regular school year. Some of the faculty members worked at either private or public schools in New England during the school year. I was the only teacher who taught at the college level. Out of the entire faculty, I was the only transplant from the city, and the biggest and most culturally diverse of them all—New York City. I was simply too young and inexperienced to adjust to the culture shock. During the three days of orientation before the students arrived, Earl Perkins covered school policy, the faculty's responsibilities, what we were to do in emergency situations, and what type of student behavior to watch out for. For the last hour or so, Earl introduced all the faculty members, returning and new alike.

When faculty introductions turned to me, Earl said that I was in the theatre, taught oral communications at several universities, and that I wrote. Earl finished my introduction by saying, "Maybe someday one of Mr. Schwartz's books will line one of the shelves in our library." Nice chap, Earl Perkins. I hope his prediction prescient.

There was a bonfire on campus that night. There were a couple of kegs. I tried circulating. I asked various faculty members about the subjects they taught. I asked about the students. I asked for tips to help me in class management. I asked if there were local bars that had live music. I remember some of the men asking me if I was married. I recall some of the women asking me what kind of car I drove. No one asked me about my teaching experiences or my writing.

The next morning at breakfast, after I filled my plate with scrambled eggs, hash brown potatoes, a few strips of bacon, and several sausage links, I scanned the cafeteria, looking for people to join. I noticed a table where six faculty members were engaged in lively conversation. There were five men and one woman. As I approached the table, the woman stopped listening to the man sitting next to her and looked up at me. Then the talking ceased entirely at the table. Everyone at the table stared at me. I could have easily sat at one of the empty tables. I chose to be social. I already sensed during the orientation period that I was regarded by more than a few with a degree of suspicion. Standing in front of that table, holding my tray, I waited in vain for someone to ask me to sit down. After I sat down, I immediately saw a shift in attitude.

At Cushing Academy, in this small New England Town, I was truly out of my realm. I was pushing forty, unmarried, without a driver's license, in the arts, and a true-blue city boy.

But not all faculty members were distant. Some of them were able to make some basic small talk now and then. And there was one married couple that I invited over to the house one night for snacks and cocktails. He taught math, and she taught biology. Yet for most of the faculty and administration, they must have thought there was something odd about me. I was sure some of them wanted me reported to the local police or committed to the nearest psycho ward when they saw me walking by myself and giggling. But I was well liked by my students, and classes were going well.

About midway through the summer session, I decided to take advantage of my spacious kitchen. I bought a few cookbooks sold at the local pharmacy in town. I bought many spices. My meatloaf was quite successful. My chicken loaf could have served as a footrest. My chili was fine but could have been more "alarming." I wouldn't serve my tuna casserole to a convicted serial killer for her last meal while she sat on death row. I went wild with salads—egg salad, potato salad, carrot salad, shrimp salad. Thank goodness for dill! I was most proud of my coleslaw, which had just a pinch of sugar in addition to the obligatory mayonnaise.

One morning, as I walked my young residents to breakfast, I advised them to eat a light dinner because, that night, I would fix them a homemade late supper. I served deviled eggs for an appetizer. For an entrée, I served my meat loaf with a side of potatoes au gratin. All fare was devoured. The Italians especially liked my meatloaf. With stuffed mouths, they said "benne," "ottimo," or "bravo" throughout the meal.

Two weeks before the end of the summer session, the summer's annual Talent Night was announced. One of my American residents occasionally strummed a guitar before turning in. I tossed him an idea. He agreed. About a week and a half later, he and I were on stage in a packed auditorium, performing a duet of the Grateful Dead's "Uncle John's Band." When our number ended, I could easily tell we drew a more enthusiastic response from the students than from faculty. The very next night, something odd and unexplainable occurred. I was sitting under a tree, reading. It was around 7:15 p.m., fifteen minutes before the campus bell rang to signify the onset of the evening study period. I heard my full name uttered. A teacher was walking toward me. In addition to teaching classes, he held a supervisory position. He also taught at Cushing Academy during the regular school year.

"Good evening," I said, closing my book.

"Good evening yourself," he said. "Come with me."

"Where to?"

"It's a surprise. C'mon."

Throughout the summer session, I hardly had any contact with him. But we did have a strange moment one afternoon in the cafeteria. I was sitting alone, the food on my tray untouched. I was feverishly writing a letter to my mother. I looked up for a moment and saw him looking at me from across the cafeteria. His expression was coolly fearful, like someone looking down at a foaming sea from a cliff before diving.

"Okay," I said, "lead the way."

Our destination turned out to be the bell tower. We ascended a musty-smelling spiral stone staircase. Then he opened the wooden door to the bell chamber.

"C'mon in. Ever ring a bell like this before?" he asked.

"Never."

"That's what I thought. Go ahead then."

I took hold of the rope.

"Just give it one good yank," he said, leaning against the wall with his arms folded.

I yanked. The bell rang several times.

"Now give it another yank."

I did.

"One more time."

I did.

"Okay," he said, "that was fine. Let's go downstairs and get some fresh air in our lungs."

"Lead the way," I said.

When we left the bell tower, I thanked him.

"My pleasure," he said.

"Quasimodo has nothing to worry about," I said.

He sucked back his cheeks in an earnest but futile attempt at smiling. At least he gave it the old college try. Three days later, I was back in New York City.

The following summer, in the July 24 issue of *The New York Times*, the following letter was published:

To the Editor:

> I agree with Heather Mac Donald (Op-Ed, July 20) that the use of "free-form progressive" methods by Teachers in the classroom insults students' intelligence.
>
> Two weeks ago I began teaching Advanced English to sixth and seventh graders at a private school with the "whole language" method. My students made journal entries based on random ideas lacking substantive context and discussed reaction to each other's writing. Apparently they "felt really comfortable," to quote a student in Ms. Mac Donald's article. It was also apparent that they were restless and bored. After three days I returned to my usual lecturing, questioning, and teaching.
>
> They are no longer bored. Maybe this is because they realize there is someone in front of them who know something they don't. My class is now a classroom, not an unfocused cafeteria.

> Laurence C. Schwartz
> New York, July 20, 1998

My stance was more reactive than prescriptive. Like some other adjuncts, I had been teaching middle school and high school students at various private institutions during winter and summer breaks. They were small businesses, not part of the public educational system. The subjects were primarily English as a Second Language, the Preliminary Scholastic Aptitude Test, and the Scholastic Aptitude Test. During the summers of '95 and '96, I taught at a summer academy named Ming Yuan in Flushing, Queens. In the morning, I taught PSAT. In the afternoon, I taught SAT, with a supplement of literature enrichment.

The students were Americanized Asians with little interest in literature, especially during the summer months. And they were difficult to manage. I was more disciplinarian than teacher. If I grouped the students with the intention of analyzing Holden Caufield's personality traits, the group discussions quickly devolved to jokes and giggles. It was only when I inhabited a stern and stoic countenance and commanded as a drill sergeant that the students paid the slightest bit of attention.

A major perk of teaching on the college level was dealing with an adult population and not worrying about managing a class or maintaining control. A vast difference existed between babysitting and teaching. Maybe if I had had children of my own, I could have coped and managed better. Of course, there are many high schools where a great deal of learning takes place, and there are many teens who are serious minded, eager for knowledge. But American teenagers will be American teenagers and there ever lurks the possibility that someone will blurt out a stupid and irrelevant remark while the teacher pursues a point. I could not abide that happening on a regular basis. Many of my peers felt the same way. A college student could very well blurt, but more times than not, it could be an intelligent and relevant remark. And I didn't want to hear bells ringing every forty minutes nor walk through overcrowded hallways nor listen to slamming lockers or pimply hyperbole.

When fall of '98 arrived, I received my usual course load from Kingsborough Community College and Long Island University, and I began to seriously miss the theatre. I paid off some back dues to Actors' Equity and started looking at the trades.

For the spring '99 semester, I accepted an additional appointment teaching a Voice and Diction course at La Guardia Community College, which was a part of the City University of New York. Sometime in early February, I auditioned for a company called Love Creek Productions. Love Creek workshopped new one-act plays and full-length plays. Its productions were Equity-approved showcases.

I landed a part in a two-character one-act play. I played a neurotic with a pathologically possessive personality. Cliff Hesse over at KCC referred me to a gentleman named Herb Wikum. Herb was the deputy chairman of the Speech Division in the College of Liberal Arts at Tobit College.

Tobit College was founded in 1971. It's the most expansive university in America with Jewish roots. The university began with a mission of focusing on higher learning for the Jewish community. Now it educates many populations. Locally, it has many sites throughout Brooklyn, Queens, and Manhattan. One of the Speech Division's offerings was a course called Interpersonal Communications. This was what Herb Wikum had in mind for me. Herb liked me well enough on Cliff's recommendation. Then Herb introduced me to a Dr. Lou Wish, an associate dean of the School of Liberal Arts. Wish hardly looked and sounded the part of associate dean. He seemed more the type you would imagine cuffing a bridegroom's tuxedo trousers in a modest tailor shop on Manhattan's Lower East Side. Dean Wish had the final say over my appointment, and he wanted full assurance that I was actively matriculating for my master's. Tobit College also has sites in Las Vegas, Los Angeles, and Tel Aviv.

Taino Towers stands in East Harlem at 123rd Street between Lexington and Third Avenue. In its basement and ground floor is a preschool. Tobit College occupies its second and third floors. Taino Towers also housed, unbeknownst to me at the time, a lovely thrust theatre with a mezzanine and plush red velvet-lined seats called Jesus Tato Laviera, where I was to direct a play some sixteen years later.

The Interpersonal Communications course should be a requirement for all seeking a degree in higher education and all high school students as well. I liked to call it Basic Psychology of Human Communication. The course basically explored what it meant to be human, with the attendant challenges, highs, lows, and problems beyond our control. More importantly, the course explored what we could strive for in ourselves, both in our professional and personal lives. It helped if the instructor had substantial life experience.

Most of my students were human service majors and planned on pursuing a branch of social work. The Interpersonal Communications course was a requirement for their degrees. They already came to the course with an invested interest, and because of this, they were more teachable and eager to master the material than my usual students in an Oral Communications class.

And if you want to be an effective social worker, you need to have superior communication skills. How do you earn someone's trust? Is it harder for a man to break free of his traditional gender role than a woman? What are the tools needed in order to become an empathetic listener? How do you build someone's self-esteem while simultaneously make them feel as if they're building it themselves? Why do some relationships grow while others stagnate? Why do certain relationships deteriorate? Have we really a choice in what our beliefs, attitudes, and values are?

But the broader question that informed the course was, why were we the way we were, and could we capitalize on our strengths while becoming more aware of our weaknesses? Anyone could benefit from taking such a marvelous course regardless of one's age, ethnicity, race, status, religion, sex, or sexual orientation.

My first class at Tobit College in Taino Towers fell on a gray March afternoon. Within the first few minutes of class, I established a warm atmosphere through the sheer excitement I had for the material. Most of the students had jobs. They also seemed world-weary and, because of this, greatly appreciated my brand of humor.

One student who hauled trash for the Department of Sanitation pounded his fist on his desk in a fit of laughter when I explained how some of the most average-looking of men could spend much more time looking at themselves in mirrors than even the vainest of Hollywood sex kittens. My point was that we often stereotyped when it came to the male and female genders.

Before I began teaching the Interpersonal Communications course, Herb Wikum had already suggested the types of written assignments to give, in addition to the traditional midterm and final. The chief assignment was called a communication journal. It contained two parts—an observation and a reflective analysis. For the observation, the student was to simply and impartially reproduce a witnessed conversation between two or more people. They could also record nonverbal behavior, like vocal tones, gestures, and facial expressions. They could also describe clothing, jewelry, and body art.

While the student observed, they could not take part in the conversation, nor could they pass judgment on the content. An observation could take place in public, in the workplace, in the student's home, or in someone else's home. For the reflective analysis, the students were to recap the observation while accurately applying specific terminology from the textbook. It was not an easy assignment to do, especially during the early weeks of the semester.

At the end of each chapter in the textbook were cases. A case consisted of a list of target terms, preview notes, and case participants. Then there followed a short scene with two and sometimes three characters. The characters' behavior was supposed to be illustrative of the target terms. The writing was clear, inoffensive, and remarkably unimaginative. I soon began writing my own scenes for students to read aloud in class and then discuss their relevance to our current lesson.

Sometime late that spring, a few of my graduate school peers and I got together one evening at a student's apartment to organize an evening of one-act plays to be written and performed by us theatre students. We reached out to the graduate students unable to make the meeting to see if they were interested in participating. We had a sense of community. It turned out to be a successful evening. The evening was held in one of Hunter College's Black Box Theaters. It was a fair-sized and receptive audience. I participated both as an actor and a playwright.

I played the role of Alexander Hamilton in Jeremy Sumpan's *Once Again in Weehawken*. The play took a broadly comic approach to the fatal duel between Arron Burr and Alexander Hamilton. Hamilton was written as a staid humbug, while Burr was portrayed as a shameless debaucher—a wry unity of opposites. The audience loved it. I wrote a one-act play called *Ida's Children*. Late middle-aged

Ida feels that her son, an unknown and unsuccessful poet, is wasting his time with trifles. Ida secretly meets with her son's lover, Lucien. Ida tries to convince Lucien to convince her son that there are more profitable endeavors that will bring both notoriety and more money while still honoring his artistic integrity. I felt that some of the lines of dialogue were truthful and offered insight into character but lacked urgency.

Like many beginning playwrights, I had an ear for dialogue but no understanding of action and conflict. Any Tom, Dick, or Harry can write a play, but to be a deft dramatist, one requires a rare and unusual skill.

The summer of '99 came, and I holidayed in County Sligo, Eire, at the home of David O'Hare. I met David during my stay at Shakespeare and Company in the summer of '94. He was a kind and gentle soul and was interested in pursuing an acting career. We shared many a conversation about theatre while strolling on the Parisian boulevards. When he arrived in New York City in the fall of '96, he contacted me. For three and a half years, he struggled to make a life for himself. He took odd jobs here and there. He never obtained a green card. He wanted to stay permanently in the United States. His maternal grandfather was born here, granting eligibility for citizenship. But records of his grandfather's birth could not be found. I even contacted a gentleman with whom I grew up in Roslyn who became an immigration judge. My efforts were for naught, and it was now time for David to return to his native land, at the government's behest. Before his sad departure, David asked me if I wanted to be his guest.

A month in the Irish countryside was plenty. David's home was walking distance to the shore, but the water only came up to my knees, and swimming was prohibited. And I swore I'd never look at another baked potato again. I was quite ready to spend my last three days in Dublin and feel city pavement under my feet.

On my second day in Dublin, I was leisurely walking down Talbot Street. I spotted a blonde coming toward me. She wore a Grateful Dead T-shirt. I approached her to say hello and introduce myself. Then I asked her if she had a favorite Grateful Dead tune. From around 1987 to Jerry Garcia's death, I was an avid Grateful Dead fan and attended many concerts. It turned out that the blonde on Talbot Street preferred Bob Dylan instead. She was a South African Jewess from Johannesburg. Samantha and I ducked into the nearest pub. It turned out that she wrote. We talked for hours. Samantha and I closed the pub. Then we walked to my hostel, where I pleasured her in my bunk bed. The next morning, we kissed before she boarded her bus. We promised to keep in touch. To this day, we maintain an active and solely epistolary relationship. Just an occasional e-mail. Simply pens and paper and postage. So rare in this age.

When I returned to New York in late July, I was nearly bust. There was barely enough in the bank to cover August's rent and the bills. I took to the streets in search of a job to see me through until after Labor Day. I walked into a Barnes & Noble outlet in Chelsea. I walked over to the prettiest sales associate I could find and asked her where I could find the manager.

"Why do you want to see the manager?"

"I'm looking for a job."

"Oh," she said as if relieved. "I'll get him. Wait here. He's around."

After a few minutes, a lanky young man wearing horn-rimmed glasses came over to me and asked, "Are you the gentleman looking for a job?

I was hired to work part-time, around twenty hours a week. The pay was twelve dollars an hour. Full-timers were paid more. I was stationed in the history section. I sold a lot of books and went out of my way to escort customers to other sections. A few times when I escorted a customer to the performing arts section, I stayed and further assisted, especially if the customer was looking for books on film and theatre. The sales associate who worked in the performing arts section was usually nowhere to be found.

When I asked the manager if I could be transferred to the performing arts section, he said, "Not now. We need someone like you in the history section." Who was someone like me?

At the end of August, I was ready to give notice. I told the manager that I was assigned more courses than expected and was unable to continue as a sales associate.

He said, "Sorry to hear that."

One of the perks of working at Barnes & Noble was the privilege of borrowing any book for ten days. I borrowed a beautiful hardcover Scribner's edition of *The Collected Short Stories of F. Scott Fitzgerald*.

When I tried to return it, the manager said, "Don't worry about it."

Ian Streicher hailed from Chicago, Illinois. I met him at Hunter College in Tina Howe's Playwrighting Workshop. We became friends. In early August '99, I approached Ian and Jeremy Sumpman—author of *Once Again in Weehawken*—with an idea. Why not the three of us coproduce an evening of one-act plays? We agreed to equally divide all expenses. We agreed to present four one-act plays on the bill. My *Ida's Children* and Jeremey's *Once Again in Weehawken*—two of them. For the remaining two, we placed an ad in Backstage. We requested the authors to send the scripts by snail mail to my address. After reading through scripts for a couple of weeks, we found our two plays. One was *Interrogation #2*. The other play centered on a troubled married couple.

We booked Wings Theatre for five consecutive evenings in mid-October. Since management already knew me at Wings Theatre from my successful reincarnation of Artaud, we were given a fair rental and able to retain a small percentage of the ticket receipts. We held an open call at Wings. By Labor Day, the plays were cast, and we decided in which order the plays were to be presented. The evening would open with *Interrogation #2*, followed by *Ida's Children*, followed by the play between the husband waxing philosophy and his bawling wife, and concluded with *Once Again in Weehawken*, wherein I resumed my role as Alexander Hamilton.

I also played one of the parts in *Interrogation #2*. He was a criminal suspect. He already confessed to the crime. He disguised himself as a UPS deliveryman in order to gain entry to a famous Hollywood starlet's high-rise apartment in Manhattan. After gaining entry, he proceeds to tie her up and verbally abuse her, decrying her unearned celebrity and fame. He declares her a talentless and shallow human being, simply a media-hyped mediocrity contributing to the hollow celebrity culture the United States has embraced. The suspect eventually dangles her out a window before dropping her to her death. The detective interrogates the suspect simply to fully comprehend the motivation behind such a heinous crime. I was adequate in the part and enjoyed playing it.

About midway through the rehearsal process, I sat down with Jeremy and Ian. We agreed to think up a general title for the evening of one-act plays. I suggested *Entangling Alliances.*

Entangling Alliances had a modestly successful five-performance run. We played to fair-sized houses. At no performance did the number of cast members exceed the number of patrons. My co-producers and I just about broke even from our meager investment. But it should be obvious to the reader and the public at large that off-off Broadway is seldom about money. It offers a different kind of enrichment. For some, it offers a diversion from the doldrums of a boring nine-to-five job. For young people fresh out of undergraduate drama programs, it offers raw experience and the glimmer of a dream to come true. For seasoned professionals long out of work and hungry for stage time, it offers the chance to flex one's acting chops. What were these experiences offering me? Two of the above and a hell of a lot of good, clean fun.

Not long after *Entangling Alliances* closed, I received a call from a director at Love Creek Productions. He asked me if I would be interested in acting in a play called *Out of the Garden.* I said yes. I was cast as one of God's singing angels. I called Lee Wilhelm, artistic director of Love Creek, and calmly asked for a larger role.

"You wanna play God?" Lee asked.

Who wouldn't want to play God?

The authors subtitled *Out of the Garden* with *A Biblical Burlesque.* There was nothing lowbrow or bawdy in the play's treatment of God, his creation Adam, or the devil. On the contrary, it was innocent, lighthearted, lyrical, literate, and warm-spirited with nary an expletive to be found in the entire script. The characters were likeable.

God has a problem. His son Adam, who resided in Eden, has turned twenty-one and has the intelligence of a six-year-old. Is he a victim of arrested development? Or is his condition the result of a too lenient and loving upbringing by his father? God seems to think the latter. God consults with the devil to pursue a strategy to mature his son Adam and equip him with the smarts and courage to leave Eden, make a life for himself, and become a man. God's assistant is the archangel Mathias, who smothers God with constant fawning.

On the day of our first company rehearsal, the actor portraying the devil had a case of halitosis that could repel a tsunami. Good thing that this was an isolated incident because the devil and I had many scenes together. Some of our scenes together were more in the style of vaudeville than burlesque, what with their wordplays, puns, and malapropisms.

While rehearsing for *Out of the Garden*, I had my one course at LIU, two courses at KCC, and now two courses at Tobit. In addition to teaching the Interpersonal Communications course at Tobit, I was offered a second course. It was basically the same remedial English course that I taught at KCC. I taught this course at Tobit's Flushing site, on Main Street, last stop on the number 7 train. It was sometimes a schlep to get there. First, I had to take a 1, 2, or 3 to Times Square. Then I would switch to the 7. The 7 could run express or local. An express was twenty minutes to the last stop, a local was twice the time.

I believe Tobit's Flushing site was once a correctional facility for women. There was a basic reception area, followed by a long hallway with windowless classrooms. All my students that first semester at Flushing were native Korean, as a good part of Flushing was dubbed Little Korea. I sensed that most of my students would not utter a word of English outside of class unless they had to. Why bother if your friends, neighbors, grocer, doctor, and everyone else in your insular orbit were Korean and would rather speak Korean rather than English, just like yourself? The students were mostly young middle-aged to elderly. They might have been taking English for the sake of their children's and grandchildren's assimilation more than their own. They accorded me with due respect and attention. Some of them even attended a performance of *Out of the Garden*, which I considered another victory of sorts, introducing them to off-off Broadway. To what degree they understood the script was an entirely different matter.

PART IV

THE CURTAIN RISES ON THE MILLENNIUM

Labe Tash, an Israeli oceanographer, is deep-sea diving a hundred miles north of Cyprus. He is searching for rare minerals for the Israeli government. Labe meets Nixie, a beautiful Asian mermaid. They are both smitten with each other. Labe brings Nixie back to Jerusalem, where a doctor scrapes off her tail to the flesh underneath. Then the doctor anaesthetizes Nixie and proceeds to give her a functioning female genitalia. Nixie has also been given the necessities that will allow her to give birth. However, the doctor fails to inform her that if she opts for reproductive surgery and gives birth, there may be side effects. One side effect may be the quick growth of a permanent beard. Another side effect may be amnesia. Nixie gives birth to Labe's child, and both side effects occur. Labe thinks it best to send Nixie to a sanitarium in Nicosia, Cyprus, where she will be tended by a private nurse. Labe will be a single father to his new son, Sire. Ten years pass, and Nixie finally recovers from her amnesia.

This is where my one-act play, *A First Family*, begins.

Nixie is enraged that the doctor failed to mention the possible side effects of giving birth. Nixie plans on filing a malpractice suit, claiming the doctor committed gross negligence. Nikos, Nixie's private nurse, tries to calm her, emphasizing all the good she has in her life, like a handsome husband and a beautiful son. Both husband and son are about to arrive to see Nixie. Labe has seen Nixie occasionally over the last ten years, but this will be the first time Nixie sees her ten-year-old son, Sire, for she became unconscious after delivering.

Underneath Nixie's anger, she fears meeting Sire. How will he react to his mother's beard? Will he let her into his life and allow her to love him after being raised solely by his father? Nikos assures Nixie, "True beauty is too often confused with a person's appearance." But Nixie is still frightened. Then she suddenly begins to remember another risk the doctor mentioned in giving birth to Labe's child. But this was a risk to the child, not Nixie. Is it congenital blindness? Then Nixie hears a child singing the following lines of the "Shepherd Boy" from Puccini's *Tosca*.

> Io de' sospiri
> Te ne rimano tanti
> Pe' quante foje
> Ne smoveno li venti

Labe enters. He asks Nixie if she can remember what the song is from.

"Tosca," she replies.

For the next few minutes, Labe rekindles some more memories, and Nixie rekindles her love for Labe. Then Nixie suddenly asks Labe who the child is whom she heard singing.

"Sire," Labe replies.

Labe exits and returns with Sire, who is blind. He is led to Nixie. He sits on Nixie's lap, feeling her hands and commenting on how soft they are.

A few moments later, Sire says, "I'm sure you're as beautiful as you sound."

Here is how the play concludes:

> NIXIE. I guess you could say I look beautiful. But I'd like to tell you something, Sire. Something you might already know, but I'll say it just the same. For both our benefits. Listening?

Sire. I am.

Nixie. Beauty…real beauty has nothing to do with a person's appearance. Right, Nikos?

Nikos. You're so right. I wish *I'd* thought of that.

I subtitled the play with *An Adult Fairytale*.

A First Family was accepted at Love Creek Productions as part of its Winter One-Acts 2000 Festival, performed at Theatre Row Studios on West 42nd Street. When I asked Lee Wilhelm if I could direct, he agreed.

For Labe, I cast Andrew Quinn, who played Burr in *Once Again in Weehawken*. For Nixie, I cast Jo Shui, whom I met in a Playwrighting Analysis class at Hunter College. For the part of Nikos, I cast a member of Love Creek, who knew the Kahns. The Kahns were from India; both were doctors. The Kahns had eight-year-old twins, Faiz and Omar. I auditioned both at the Kahns' apartment. Faiz was the better actor, but he couldn't sing. Omar sang beautifully. I cast Faiz as on-stage Sire and Omar as off-stage singing Sire. I hope that wherever the Kahn twins are today, the experience they had in *A First Family* leaves even the faintest of smiles.

I'd never taken a Directing class. Directing was a completely new experience. I was able to relate well to the actors. I already had a sense of stage business, staging, and the use of space. And my actors were quite good. The Kahn twins were a dream. After our three performances, I knew that *A First Family* touched its audience. You would have to be made of stone not to be touched by the sight of a blind child.

On an overcast mid-August Saturday morning in 1970, my father took me to see the New York Giants practice at Hofstra University, Long Island. Hofstra University was a client of my father's. After the morning's scrimmage ended, my father and I rose from the stands and proceeded to take a leisurely walk around campus. We eventually made our way to a dining hall, where the New York Giants were lunching. They certainly seemed like a talkative bunch. Then a mountain of a man was suddenly standing beside me. He looked older than the rest of the players and seemed a bit sad.

"Oh, Mr. Webster!" my father said.

"This is my son Larry. Larry, say hello to Alex Webster."

Mr. Webster turned to me and held out his hand. When I shook it, a moment passed before I could gather some words. My fingers felt like they were wrapped in thick sausage links.

"Hello, Mr. Webster," I said.

"Hello, Larry."

I'd just shaken hands with the head coach of the New York Giants.

In the early morning of August 31, 2000, while sleeping, my father died of a massive coronary. Less than a week later, it was my very first day teaching a Speech Communications course at Hofstra University.

They say that you never really appreciate someone or something until you go without. It could be a limb, a reliable dope dealer, your eyesight, or a mouse-free apartment. So was the case with my Hofstra University students. This was a middle-class, suburban student population, and until that point in my teaching career, they were my students with the highest caliber. Their writing skills were reflective of a college student. They mastered basic grammar, syntax, and spelling. They were always prompt to class, consistently present, had the widest attention span, and were the most verbal. Some of them even read a newspaper. They had a working grasp of history. They were the easiest to engage in open discussions. Alas, I should have capitalized on these perks.

What I recently learned was that a key component of an Oral Communications class should be engaging the students in open discussions on any given topic. The instructor could choose quite the variety. The more a student willingly participated in an open discussion, the higher odds that said student would get over this deep-rooted American fear of public speaking. Alas, my style of teaching at Hofstra was more the traditional lecture. I always tried to deliver interesting lectures, but a student's appreciation of an entertaining and informative lecture was no indication of learning.

I had ammunition with my Hofstra students for conversation and eliciting different voices and attitudes, but like a fool, I failed to use it. Many students read the chapters the dates they were assigned, a rarity among my community college students, unless, of course, I scheduled a quiz. Many students had their own version of reading a chapter for class. This consisted of scanning the chapter five or ten minutes before class began. Many of my Hofstra students read the chapter before class began and had given the content some thought. When this occurred, it benefitted both the instructor and the student.

Fall of 2000 went well for me at Hofstra, yet I was quite surprised when the secretary of the Department of Speech and Rhetorical Studies asked me for my availability to teach for spring of 2001. I was offered the same two-section course load. I graciously accepted. But all was not rosy. The one literal and figurative cost of teaching at Hofstra that outweighed the rewards was that blasted commute.

My commute started with a short subway ride to Pennsylvania Station. Then I boarded the Long Island Rail Road for a twenty-minute ride to Jamaica, Queens. Then I transferred to the Hempstead line for Hofstra University. After arriving in Hempstead station, I rode a crowded shuttle bus to campus. Many a morning I arrived fried and frazzled from the commute. That shuttle bus was a literal pain in the arse. Without any traffic at all, it was a ten-minute ride. It was a traditional school bus, so when you sat down, you could feel the knotted metal underneath. And it was a bumpy ride. I always taught morning classes. The shuttle was always standing room only. Getting a seat was always a gamble. You could feel the tension. And it always seemed that the faculty were standing and the students sitting. From my door to Hofstra's campus, it was a good hour and a half commute, the last twelve or so minutes on that dreaded shuttle. To this very day, I assign the foulest of meanings to the word *shuttle*.

I taught at Hofstra two days a week. The commute cost around 125 dollars a month. It was a lovely campus, with red and brown brick structures with easily navigable interiors, beautifully manicured lawns, and a particularly fetching statue of Copernicus. One early fall sun-drenched morning, I emerged from the campus library, a couple of newly borrowed books under my arm, feeling unexpectedly integrated with an earned sense of belonging.

I began spring of 2001 with two courses at Hofstra and three courses at Tobit. I had since lost my appointments at CUNY.

Sometime during the early part of 2001, I submitted my play *Ida's Children* to the off-off Broadway company Theatre-Studio Inc. It was accepted for a three-performance run. I decided to direct it. For the part of Ida, I cast Eve Sorrel. Eve stage-managed *Max's Millions*, and she was also a very capable actress. For the part of Ida's son's companion, I cast one of my Hofstra students. I could tell early on that Tom was troubled. One day, the topic of discussion turned to stage acting, and I noticed at once that his expression lightened. I asked him if he was interested in theatre, and he said, "Yes, I am." I asked him if he ever performed, and he said, "Yes, I have."

For his informative speech, Tom spoke about how fairy tales could have a morally instructive effect on children. As a primary source of information, he used, at my suggestion, Bruno Bettelheim's *The Uses of Enchantment*, which I had read some years earlier. Tom quoted both Bettelheim and Piaget during his speech. He won me over. I asked him to read from the script one afternoon, and he was fine. He accepted the part. He was quite good. He made my writing sound better than it was.

Summer of 2001 found me unemployed but hardly idle. I spent a good deal of time at my girlfriend's apartment in Flushing, Queens. I spent my time cultivating my relationship with my girlfriend's eight-year-old daughter, eating her mother's Korean cuisine, writing short fiction, and composing doggerel. I filed an unemployment insurance claim in June, so I had enough income to stay afloat. It was the longest stretch of unemployment in my professional life.

The Harry Van Arsdale Jr. Center of Labor Studies is a division of the State University of New York at Empire State College. The Van Arsdale Center coordinates a partnership with certain civic and labor organizations. One of these organizations is the International

Brotherhood of Electrical Workers, Local #3. This is the electrician's union. To join the union, you need to fulfill certain requirements, like accumulating a certain number of working hours as a Journeyman, which is another term for *apprentice*. Journeymen put in full-time hours.

Another requirement is to earn a certain number of college credits. Three of these credits are from a College Writing course. Why an electrician must show proficiency in writing a college-level essay before qualifying for union membership only the gods of profit can say. So there I was, in the fall of 2001, in a public middle school in Chelsea, standing before a large class of early to mid twentysomething journeymen electricians. They were to learn about the informative and persuasive essay. They were to learn the effective use of paragraph development, grammar, syntax, and style. Are these skills needed to rewire a chandelier's circuit? I arrived to class in a foul humor because I had just commuted from Hofstra.

They were a friendly and uncontrollable mob. They immediately recognized in me an easy mark to take advantage of. Except for one young man who I learned was devoutly religious, none of them took the class very seriously. I did. Big mistake. I was young and naïve, still lacking the ability to coast through a course while still fulfilling its objectives. In order to do that, you need to be seasoned, apathetic, or a tenured professor—or all the above.

Except for a couple of butch lesbians who sat together, the students were men. About two weeks into the semester, I began to realize that more than a few of the men came to class with a beer buzz on. I could smell the beer on their breaths as they entered the classroom, giggling and jostling one another. What probably started out as a beer or two before class grew into three or four after they realized what a softy I was. I'd stand in front of the chalkboard, discussing the use of adverbs or what a topic sentence was, and then someone would blurt a completely irrelevant remark, getting a chuckle or two. Then someone else would follow up with a complimentary remark and garner a few more chuckles. Then came the topper from another student, this time getting a laugh from most of the class. What a joke.

Looking back, why blame them for lack of discipline? Being an electrician requires skill and intelligence, but it should not, I believe, require the discipline to earn three credits from a College Writing course. They did not want to be there. After a while, I joined in on the joke. I even stopped trying to discuss writing technique. I simply gave them in-class writing exercises. One time, a couple of students, half-drunk, started talking to one another during a writing exercise.

I politely told them, "Put off the talking until after class, and try to complete the exercise."

They complied with my request for about a minute before resuming their chatter. Then I looked at them and deliberately stage-whispered, "Psst!" They stopped talking and looked at me, as did the rest of the class.

Then I addressed them as a fearful convict would address a stern judge before being sentenced. "I asked you nicely once. Now I'm going to tell you nicely. Shut up. Close the holes underneath your noses. Please. Shut up. Shut up and write. You don't want to see me angry."

I knew before making this pronouncement that I would not return to this position in the spring. It paid crap, and I had Hofstra and Tobit as my bread and butter. After looking around at their fellow journeymen for support and receiving none, then looking at me and trying to think of a comeback, the two chattering students picked up their pens and focused on their assigned task. Then I noticed our devoutly religious journeyman nodding at me with benedictional approval.

It was after this incident that the class and I worked out an unwritten social contract. They would be more disciplined so long as I took the class less seriously. We worked out a workable rapport. Thereafter, I found out that one of the students liked Wagner. He was an amiable Long Island boy and worked as an auxiliary fire fighter on weekends. I lent him my Deutsche Grammophon compact disc edition of *Wagner's Overtures* to duplicate. I have since pictured him speeding to a class C fire in the dead of night while listening to the "Ride of the Valkyries."

After the last night of class, around ten journeymen and I went to a pub in the Meatpacking District. It was a spot known to be popular with the local biking community. I was treated to several drinks and a chicken fingers appetizer. My fellow Wagner enthusiast bought me my first of many rounds.

It was around this time that I returned to playing the suspect in *Interrogation #2*. The artistic director of Theatre-Studio Inc. liked *Ida's Children*, so after I sent her a copy of *Interrogation #2*, she agreed to letting me perform on any Friday and Saturday night. I was joined by the original detective from the Wings Theatre production. I was teaching, acting, and writing short fiction. It had been almost a year and a half since Hunter College's departmental brass approved my graduate thesis proposal. I had completed all my required credits and passed both the comprehensive and language exams. The language exam required the translation of Antonin Artaud from Spanish to English. I suppose it was common knowledge to senior faculty in the Theatre Department that I was an Artaudian. Now all I needed to earn my MA was to complete my thesis. It would be another good four years before this became a reality. Could I have been creating an art form for procrastination?

By April 2002, I started looking for summer work. I found an ad in *The New York Times*, seeking counselors and "teachers" for the upcoming summer session at Camp Mohawk. I called the number listed and arranged an interview with Mohawk's director.

Camp Mohawk is in White Plains, about an hour's drive north of Manhattan. I took a bus and a short cab ride to the interview. It was a rainy and raw afternoon, hardly the setting for a summer day camp. The camp's offices were in a small house. I was wet and cold when I turned the doorknob. The camp director looked at my résumé and made an innocuous comment about voice and diction. I wondered who the bigger fool was—the director for hiring me or me for accepting his offer.

The first night of orientation fell on a lovely late mid-June afternoon. The pickup point for the bus to transport staff was on the Upper East Side, in front of a church. I was the first to arrive. I sat on the church steps, summoning a positive attitude. A lanky red-haired teenager stopped in front of the church steps. He took a piece of paper from his pants pocket, then looked the church up and down. Then he started up the church steps. He was around twenty feet to my left, so when I greeted him, I was sure to speak up. He ignored me. When he sat down, he pulled out his portable disc player and proceeded to put in the earplugs. I got up and crossed the street. I looked at him. He gloomily stared straight ahead of him, bereft of both surroundings and passersby.

A few hours later, as sundown yielded to dusk, I was sitting in a barn-like structure, listening to Mohawk's director prattle on about camp rules, regulations, and policy. He continued to take ten minutes in covering a matter that could be explained in two. Occasionally, he told stories about emergencies that occurred at Camp Mohawk and how through the diligence and dedication of its staff, serious injury was averted. He delivered this lecture standing beside a flip chart. I tried to listen, but my mind kept drifting off. I felt like sucking on a hemlock leaf. There I was, almost forty-one years old, listening to a summer day camp director warn me about the dangers of peanut oil and how it could be fatal to someone with an allergic reaction.

Of the many mistakes I've made in my life, accepting the position of head counselor at Camp Mohawk takes center stage.

I smelled trouble. I overslept on the morning of orientation day for parents and campers. I arrived almost an hour late. I joined Jerome, my assistant counselor, who was having a conversation with some camp parents. Jerome was Black. After introducing myself as head counselor and referring to Jerome as my assistant, he looked at me as if I'd just burned down an orphanage during Sunday morning church services.

On the very first day of camp, upon arrival, I was demoted to assistant counselor. I said, "Okay." Then I was instructed to go to a certain group. The group consisted of nine-year-old boys. I worked with this group for about two weeks, doing what I was told—standing in the outfield while the boys played soft ball, standing in a swimming pool while the boys swam laps, standing on a tarred basketball court under a merciless sun, retrieving tennis balls, and watching the boys eat their camp lunches. I never had a cross word with any of the counselors or administration, and the boys liked me.

One morning, I was informed that I was now a "floater." This meant that whenever a camp activity was short on staff, yours truly would dutifully fill in. I was directed to go to arts and crafts. I prayed to stay there for the rest of the summer. I was around cool clay bricks, watercolors, assorted brushes, and lots of water. It was my oasis in a desert. My prayers went unanswered. After only three days, they moved me to archery. I remember archery only because the head instructor, a young middle-aged man, incessantly spoke on his cell phone to a doctor about his mother's deteriorating condition. Sometimes he raised his voice and said, "We've been through this, Doctor. I want new news, not old."

I might have been able to abide this grueling eight-and-a-half-hour day had it not been for another grueling commute. I rose at 7:00 a.m. each morning. At 7:30 a.m., I boarded a mini school bus a short distance from my apartment in the West Village. Some parents placed their children on the bus. This was the morning's first pickup point. From there, we made our way to the Westside Highway. Then we made two more pickups in Bronxville, where we were joined by more children and a few early twentysomething counselors. Then we made our way back to the Westside Highway. We arrived at camp a few minutes before 9:00 a.m. By then, I was in no condition to put in an eight-and-a-half-hour day under a scorching sun.

The air conditioner in the mini school bus was broken. Every day, the temperature seemed to reach the nineties. These were the early days of global warming. After the first few days of camp, I went to the administrative office and informed a teenaged receptionist about the broken air conditioner. Two days passed, and still nothing was done. The bus's windows would only open a crack. There was no relief. The children were suffering as well. I went back to the administrative office and asked to see the director. This was during my half-hour lunch break. The receptionist told me he was "in conference" but that I could wait.

That afternoon, I pulled one of the division heads aside, an orthodox Jew who consumed nothing but home-brought egg salad each day for lunch. I calmly explained about the air conditioner, emphasizing how it seemed to be affecting the children. I asked him if he could be so kind as to mention this to the director or someone who worked in operations.

He nodded his head and said, "I'll do what I can. Give me a day or so."

Two days passed, and nothing was done. I arrived at camp light-headed, with dampened underwear and a sweat-soaked polo shirt. Staff wasn't allowed to wear T-shirts. The next morning, on the way to camp, I was sitting next to a blond-haired little boy. He couldn't have been more than six. Throughout the ride, he wriggled in his seat and sighed a lot.

"You're hot, aren't you?" I asked.

"Yeah. I'm hot."

"Why don't you tell your dad or mom tonight that you're hot on the camp bus? Or maybe you can tell your mom and dad at dinner that the bus has no air conditioner."

The boy looked out the window. Then he configured a circle on it with his pinky. "I'm gonna do that. At dinner."

After I woke up the next morning, I took my usual vitamin C tablet. I boarded the bus, holding a large bottle of iced-cold Evian, breaking a sacred rule: "Absolutely no food or beverage of any kind on the bus." When I got off the bus after we pulled into camp, one of the frumpy "greeters" noticed my bottle of Evian.

"Excuse me," she said. "You're not allowed any water or food on the bus."

"I know," I said, "but the air conditioner is broken. I've told management, but nothing has been done. I need water. Do you want me fainting on the bus from sun stroke? It might unsettle the children." I turned and walked away.

That afternoon, instead of eating lunch, I walked over to the infirmary, which was air-conditioned.

"Can I help you?" the nurse asked.

"I'm feeling a little dizzy. I just want to sit here for a spell. Okay?"

She pursed her lips and shrugged her shoulders. After ten minutes, she stood up from her desk and entered a back room. She closed the door behind her. When she returned, she formed an eerily transparent smile. Then the infirmary door opened, and one of the division heads walked in. He wore a white cap, held a mask, and wore a superhero cape. He stood there and looked at me, obviously searching for the right words to use.

I interceded and said, "It's cool in here. I'm using my half-hour lunch break to sit here, where it's nice and cool."

He looked at the nurse, then looked at me. "Oh. Okay," he said. Then he turned and waddled away, his cape draping the cool wooden floor.

That night, I received a call from the camp director. He used the term "parting of the ways." I felt flattered that he dismissed me using a hackneyed yet poetic turn of phrase. He could have said, "Don't bother coming into camp tomorrow. I'm letting you go." Or he could have had one of his minions do it. I vowed never to work in a summer camp again. But it was a vow I couldn't keep.

In the fall of 2002, my short story "Catch of the Day" was published in an online magazine, *The Pink Chameleon*.

"Catch of the Day" is my vision of my parents' courtship. When the story opens, my mother is still unsure of marrying the man she has been seeing for over a year. The story's last sequence finds our young couple sitting in a darkened balcony in a New York City movie theatre in the late fifties. A cartoon is playing on screen to preview the evening's feature. There's only one member of the adult audience who's laughing at the action on screen, and he's our heroine's beau. It's at that moment that our heroine decides to marry her steady fella.

I printed out a copy of "Catch of the Day" that was headed by the e-zine's logo and concluded with my short bio containing my faculty status at Hofstra University. I placed the story in Dr. Field's mailbox at Hofstra. Field chaired the Department of Speech Communication and Rhetorical Studies. Field and I rarely spoke. When I saw him later that semester at a departmental meeting, he didn't mention my story, and I didn't bother asking him about it. I was grateful to Field for one thing—using the word *luddite* at one of our departmental meetings. It was the very first time I'd heard the word. I believe that had I been living during the early stages of the Industrial Revolution, I would have been a card-carrying luddite.

It wasn't until fall 2002 that I'd been given some shared office space at Hofstra. There were colleges that would not even grant their adjuncts any office space whatsoever; Tobit College was among them. I met an adjunct much younger than I. He was in his late twenties, having already earned his graduate degree. He told me he planned on returning to school to earn his doctorate in theology. He also told me about his summer job, working in a Long Island vineyard. Now, whenever the young man comes to mind, I can think of scripture and wine. By spring of 2003, our future theologian had departed the grounds of Hofstra University. I had the office space to myself. It was unwelcomed privacy. This changed the following fall when I met Dan Flickstein.

Dan and I hit it off right away. Dan was a retired public school teacher. Now he had a pension coming in. Not a bad deal. Dan also taught at Brooklyn College. Dan especially liked the way I spoke and counseled students who'd come into the office during my designated office hours. I'd usually talk to them about their progress in the course or how to strengthen their weaknesses or about upcoming assignments. On rare occasions, a student would ask me about career choices. To one student who was interested in pursuing a film directing career, I said, "Follow the dream, but be practical." Dan Flickstein witnessed this pseudo sagacity and nodded his head in approval.

By now I'd become one of Herb Wikum's darlings at Tobit College. He observed me in class and appreciated my style of teaching and my enthusiasm. I could depend on Herb assigning me three, sometimes four, classes per semester. I was usually assigned one section of the Interpersonal Communications course. These were my better students at Tobit. They were usually upperclassmen, majoring in human services. Most Interpersonal Communications sections met once a week in the evening, which meant that most of, if not all, the students worked full-time. Many of them worked in the educational systems, either as administrators or assistant teachers.

My other courses at Tobit were Public Speaking, A Survey of Human Communications, or Remedial English. Some of the students in these courses did not belong in a college classroom. Their personal or professional lives could have prevented adequate commitment. Or they lacked the concentrative skills. Or they lacked the basic reading and writing skills. The division for which I taught at Tobit maintained an open admission policy. The admission procedure consisted of filling out a short application. Should a student have difficulty answering a question, administration would gladly assist. I'd witnessed an administrator translating the questions into a student's native language while the student's parent watched. I'd read papers from quite a few Tobit students that betrayed functional illiteracy. The syntax, spelling, and grammar were alarmingly atrocious. Most of the students at this level were the products of the New York City public school system, were non-native speakers, or both.

I am convinced that I've had Tobit students who have never read an entire novel, a play, or a short story. I don't know their acumen for math or science, but in terms of history, I've had classes where I've mentioned names like Roosevelt and Churchill to nary a hint of recognition. I believe that this level of student does not read the assigned chapters not so much from laziness than an inability to understand and digest the information. Never mind that they have nothing to say when an instructor tries to engage them in discussion. It didn't take me long to understand just how much I needed to dumb down the material for certain students. Mind that I'm describing these students in terms of academic ability, not as people. I've met plenty of PhDs with hearts of stone.

Some of my sections at Tobit were ridiculously small, with anywhere from three to five students. One time, I taught a Remedial English class to a trio of young Hispanic women. They were all in their early twenties. Class began at nine in the morning. This wasn't so much remedial English as it was beginning ESL. And that was exactly how I taught the class. Instead of guiding them through essay writing, I taught basic grammar and conversational skills. I'd break for ten minutes at 10:30 a.m. At 10:50 a.m., the young ladies would return to class, carrying takeout breakfasts they'd purchased at a nearby deli. There they sat side by side in the last row of the class, having giggly conversations in Spanish over their bacon and eggs. I did not protest. By then, I'd learned that as some of my students were the bottom of the barrel, so, too, was Tobit's administration. I didn't want advice. I wanted action.

Another adjunct at Tobit once told me that she tried to appeal to the dean of faculty to remove a student from one of her classes because the student would fall asleep and loudly snore for most of the class. Her phone calls and e-mails to the dean of faculty went unanswered. Unless a student posed a genuine physical threat or attended class under the influence of drugs or alcohol or was wildly difficult to manage, Tobit administration or its site directors would not intervene. Why should intervention and the weeding of unacceptable behavior and poor academic performance occur at an institution with so low a standard for admission? To be sure, there were divisions and classes at Tobit College with much higher caliber students who were held accountable. Not so with the Speech Department.

And then there was my experience at Sunset Park. Sunset Park was one of Tobit's shabbier sites. I took the N train to Queens and got off at Fifty-Third Street. Then I walked up a steep Fifty-Third to a ramp that led to the building's front door. Then I walked up two flights of stairs to the dreariest excuse of a college environment the academic world over. No climbing ivy here. No busts of Demosthenes or Cicero. Just a fluorescent-lit main floor randomly branched by small and windowless classrooms.

One semester, I taught a morning Public Speaking class. There were only three students, a trio of young Black women. It was one of those ridiculously small classes, but they were serious young women who focused. One of them planned on practicing medicine. The class met once a week. About five weeks into the semester, at around 9:45 a.m., a young man appeared at the door. He looked at me and waved.

"Can I help you?" I asked.

He reached into his pocket and removed a pink receipt. I checked the receipt. He was in the right class.

"Good morning," I said. "Please sit down. I'll give you a course syllabus at the end of class." He blinked several times, then tiptoed his way to a seat and sat down.

I already suspected there was something wrong. After he sat down, he looked at the floor. He entered class while I was discussing potential topics for a short informative speech. I brought the young man up to date. I started discussing famous and infamous people. I began with names like Jonas Salk, Idi Amin, John Wilkes Booth, Arthur Ashe, Coco Chanel, and Walt Whitman. I turned my attention to the young woman with dreams of practicing medicine and asked her who *she* thought was a worthy subject for a short speech.

"Maya Angelou," she replied.

"Very good," I said. "You can discuss her poetry, her prose, or her activism, but not all three. It's only a five-minute speech."

Then I looked at the young man and asked him the very same question. "Who do you think is a worthy subject for a short college classroom speech?"

He didn't respond. I went to my desk and picked up his receipt. I repeated the question, addressing him by his surname. He slowly raised his head and rotated it in a circular motion. Then he gave me a look that fell nothing short of sheer idiocy. His eyes lit up. His expression betrayed the dubious combination of perverse gratitude for having been asked a question and an almost joyous inability to answer it. It gave me the shivers.

Then he uttered, "Huh?"

This was not a matter of a learning disability. He could have been under the influence of strong medication. Or he could have been a special needs student in high school. I wouldn't put anything past Tobit's Admissions Department. How should a teacher respond in such a situation? I wouldn't allow myself a third turn at repeating the question lest I lost what little dignity I had left. I continued the discussion with my other students for a few more minutes before dismissing the class for a ten-minute break. After the young ladies left the classroom, my new student stood up, took a deep breath, waved at me, and left the room. When class resumed, our young man did not return. He never again returned.

Then there was the bizarre experience I had at Tobit's Flushing site. I was teaching an Interpersonal Communications class. It was a small class but large enough to generate active discussion. There were maybe nine or ten students, all Black women. One of them drove a bus for the MTA, and she wore her uniform to class. They were all relatively serious students, and most did their weekly homework. It was one of my better classes. About four weeks into the semester, a young Black gentleman joined us. He was probably Jamaican. He had a hulking presence. He sat at a distance from the rest of the class, in the back row. He always looked straight ahead of him, and his upper body would now and then undulate. Whenever I asked him a question, he'd shoot back a relevant answer that indicated he was reading the chapters. Some weeks later, he submitted his first communication journal.

You'll recall that the communication journal consisted of two parts—an observation and a reflective analysis. For the observation, the writer would impartially describe a communicative encounter that he witnessed but was not directly involved in. For the reflective analysis, he would apply various terminology that bore relevance to the encounter. When I read our young man's communication journal, I saw that his observation took place in a London Discotheque. In graphic detail, he went on to describe dancing, flirting, drinking, and discreetly snorting cocaine under the ceiling's revolving strobe. Then he described a masked man bursting onto the scene and opening fire using an automatic rifle. Bodies began to fall, and blood splattered the walls and dance floor. Then the gunman fled. In the reflective analysis, our unharmed narrator took flight and gave chase to the gunman through the streets of London's West End amid whaling sirens and stunned onlookers, along Oxford Street passed Tottenham Court Road. At Marble Arch, our narrator finally caught up to the sprinting gunman, wrestled him to the ground, seized the weapon, and pointed it at the gunman's forehead until several LPD squad cars arrived on the scene.

The journal was extremely well written, with perfect grammar and spelling. The student could have been suffering from mental illness, or he could have misunderstood the assignment. Even though it was a well-written paper, the incident unsettled me. There was also his erratic behavior in class. I reported it to the administration. It turned out that the student in question had a criminal background.

A private detective was called in to roam the halls during the evening my class met.

I've had my share of Tobit students with criminal backgrounds. One student openly admitted that he'd done time. I didn't ask what the crime was. There were also a few homeless students who were living in city shelters. I've always thought of myself as just as much a champion of the underdog as the next fellow; it's just that it can be somewhat disconcerting in an academic context.

One morning, I was at Tobit's site in Bensonhurst, Brooklyn. I asked a Russian administrator about a problem with the Xerox machine, and she stridently replied, "Eeeeeez no' my job! Eeeeeez no' my job!" Every semester, you would have to pray that your paperwork was processed on time so that you could be paid on the first payroll cycle and not wait for the second or even the third. The glorified walk-in closets administration referred to as "bookstores" could often lag in stocking your textbook until weeks into the semester. Once, on the very first evening of the semester at Tobit's Manhattan site, there were no available classrooms. I held my class in the lounge, surrounded by vending machines and two janitors noisily chowing down their Big Macs and fries. One of them burped.

You keep a stiff upper lip and onward march, secure in the knowledge that this is not Alfred Jarry's College de Pataphysique but Albert Camus's University of the Absurd.

In late spring of 2003, I had another short story published in the online journal *The Paumanok Review*. "Rabbi Soloman's Court" is about an adjunct who is in between the fall and spring semesters. He takes a job teaching for the most fundamentalist Hasidic sect in New York City, the Satmar. He is hired to teach four afternoons a week at a Shul in Williamsburg, Brooklyn. His students arc fifth graders. The class begins at 3:30, after the students have spent the last six hours on vigorous sectarian studies. On the very first day of class, our adjunct quickly learns that he is quite incapable of managing and disciplining a class of twenty-five little hyperactive prepubescent Hassidic boys who cannot sit still and listen. The narrator *and* I lasted a week.

In the fall of 2004, my colleague over at Hofstra, Dan Flickstein, used his position at Brooklyn College to have me reappointed in the Speech Department. It felt good to be back at BC and earning CUNY's wages. On my very first morning back at BC, all twenty-two students were on time and ready to take notes. Within minutes, Dan stopped in the hallway, in front of the classroom. I made quick eye contact, and Dan approvingly smiled. It was one of the sweeter moments in my life as an adjunct and most likely the sweetest moment an adjunct could have.

Two days a week, I taught at three campuses: Brooklyn College in Flatbush, Hofstra University in Hempstead, and Tobit College in midtown Manhattan. I taught two very early morning Public Speaking classes at Brooklyn College. Then I rode the number 2 subway train to Atlantic Avenue. Then I boarded the Long Island Rail Road for Jamaica, Queens, where I changed for the train to Hempstead. I taught my two sections at Hofstra, whiled away an hour or so, caught the Hofstra shuttle back to Hempstead Station, and boarded a 4:30 p.m. Jamaica-bound train then switched for the train to Pennsylvania Station. I arrived at Penn Station amid the thick of rush-hour madness and scurried through the horde and up to street level, where another horde awaited me. Then I bobbed and weaved through the horde to Tobit College to teach my 6:00 p.m. class, shaken and baked from the day's commutes.

All three colleges offered quite different student populations. This is another challenge to the Adjunct who teaches at several schools. It's often necessary to adapt different styles and levels of instruction suited for the kind of student sitting in front of you. I hadn't been teaching long enough to rise to the challenge. Or perhaps I was unwilling to rise to the challenge.

I knew that spring of 2005 would be my final semester at Hofstra University. Dan Flickstein had since left. Maybe I would have continued if my work was acknowledged or welcomed. From administrators to full-time tenured faculty members and department and division secretaries, there was never a "Hello, Instructor" or a "How are you?" or a "How are classes going?" If I had a question for one of the secretaries in the Division of Liberal Arts, I felt like I was intruding. I'd say, "Good morning," and both secretaries would look at me, waiting for me to state my business.

It can be demoralizing and dispiriting to make a long and lonely commute to a place where you're worse than invisible. For to be invisible, you had to have once existed. You feel more like a nonentity. I was tired of this feeling, tired of the commute, and tired of spending over 100 dollars a month on train fare. Hofstra was all around the most prestigious institution I'd served. And there were for sure gifted faculty members who'd written books on a variety of subjects that were of interest to me—subjects like film, philosophy, and literary criticism. But I felt that this distinguished faculty were members of a club to which I was not welcome. I did learn to refine my technique and gained a good deal of confidence in the classroom. But it takes a skin thicker than mine to have otherwise continued in such a climate.

In the late spring of 2005, I was offered to teach a summer session for one of the finest and oldest educational institutions in the world—Phillips Exeter Academy. I had sent my résumé to several New England private academies. I got a call from PEA's summer session director, Doug Rogers. After listening to me describe my teaching methods and a little bit about my summer at Cushing Academy, he offered me two morning sections of Public Speaking, and one morning section of the Art of Debate. I accepted. I left a message with my chair at Hofstra, who had successfully coached and toured with Hofstra's debating team. I needed some quick schooling and advice. My message went unanswered. I ordered an instructional manual written by the University of Vermont's Edwin W. Lawrence Professor of forensics, Professor Alfred C. "Tuna" Snider.

The formal application to PEA seemed endless, and I had to undergo a thorough criminal background check. No doubt *these* young people *did* read novels and discuss plays and *did* know something of American and world history and could probably wipe the floor with me in matters of math and science. But alas, I failed to capitalize on these students' level of education or abilities. Can I offer the excuse that my experience with some Tobit students kept me from rising to the occasion? Could it be traced to my lack of experience? On hindsight, it could have been both. It seemed a pattern was taking place. When given a better brand of student, I failed to capitalize on it.

Prior to the students' arrival at the PEA summer session, there were two days of orientation for staff and faculty. At the end of the orientation, Doug Rogers introduced all the faculty members. We were instructed to stand and share what subject we'd be teaching. After we all stood and introduced ourselves, we all gave one another a round of applause. Then everyone walked over to the main dining hall for cocktails and a sumptuous buffet. I walked over and introduced myself to Kenneth Butler, who'd be teaching drama. When I told him about my theatre background, he asked me if I would be interested in joining him in directing the afternoon drama students in an evening of short scenes to be performed at the end of the summer session.

Rehearsals were held in the late afternoons. Ken and I each directed two scenes. I had a multiracial cast. The strongest moments in my scenes were between a lady of means rebuffing the romantic overtures of a military officer. Both parts were played by Black students, and both had wonderfully natural talents. I gave them precise staging directions and pacing. I made a few brief remarks about character.

On the afternoon that followed our first of two performances, there was a school assembly after lunch. Doug Rogers made a couple of announcements about preparations for student departures. Then he announced that he'd attended the previous night's performance of short scenes. I saw him sitting alone a few rows in front of me. He looked extremely pensive throughout the evening. When he began speaking about the performance, he used adjectives like *phenomenal* and *magnificent*. And he did so with a somber tone of voice. I wasn't sure whether he was sincere or merely following school protocol for the purpose of filing seats. Maybe he was sincere. Enclosed in the envelope containing my final paycheck, there was an additional check to the sum of twenty-five dollars. On the line next to memo were the words "Bonus for directing."

This was the very first of many future payments I'd receive for stage directing.

In late August 2005, I received a letter of warning from Hunter College's Graduate Theatre Department. Either I completed my thesis by the end of the upcoming academic year, or I would be permanently suspended from the program. It was a thoroughly justified letter. It had been five and a half years since departmental approval of my thesis proposal and twelve years since I began matriculating. In June 2006, I completed my thesis and earned my MA in Theatre. I haven't officially confirmed it, but I'm sure I hold the record for taking the longest time to earn an MA. It's not as dubious an achievement as having earned the lowest score nationwide on the math section of the SAT, but it certainly holds its own. And it's a good thing that I earned my MA when I did. For in late August 2006, I received a call from Paul Trent. Paul was the director of the Speech Division in the Media Studies Department at Mercy College. I had sent Mercy a résumé. We arranged an interview.

At Grand Central Station, I boarded the Metro North's Croton-Harmon line. When the train pulled out of the tunnel, my first stop was Harlem at 125th Street. The next stop was Yankee Stadium. Then it was not long before I was riding along the beautiful sun-kissed Hudson River and then arrived at the Ardsley-on-Hudson stop. Now I was in Dobbs Ferry, a suburb of Westchester County. On the platform, I saw a large white sign that read Mercy College in coal-black letters. I crossed and walked down a few steps. Then I walked up a steep, winding road sandwiched by ascending underbrush to my left and sloping underbrush to my right that overlooked the Hudson. When I reached the campus, to my left, I saw a small porched colonial. This served as office space for Mercy's Media Studies Department. A country quaint setting followed an idyllic commute.

Like many an interview I'd been on before and since, it was more a requisite formality than a genuine screening for viable job candidates. This is one of the perks of navigating the adjunct jungle. When you receive a call or an e-mail from a chair or a chair's secretary, they usually want to fill the position as soon as possible. So when you are interviewed and you speak well with a degree of authority and expertise, you're hired. At least this has been my experience.

I had a pleasant interview with Paul Trent, and it was conducted by a gentleman. I was hired to teach a single section of Oral Communications, by now my bread-and-butter course. My class met on Sunday afternoons at Mercy's Manhattan campus, on 66 West Thirty-Fifth Street, just east of Herald Square. I had absolutely no notion that Mercy College would eventually turn out to be a saving grace.

I was reappointed to Brooklyn College for the fall of 2006. I knew that BC had a reputable Theatre Department. Now that I had my master's, I decided to contact the chairman of the Theatre Department. I e-mailed him a letter of interest and attached a résumé. And of course, I mentioned that I'd been teaching for the BC Speech Department. He promptly returned my e-mail and wrote that he'd be happy to meet with me.

When I entered his office, he immediately projected a hollow good cheer that rang false. His manner seemed pat and canned. He had a pronounced New York dialect, dropping the *R* at the ends of words. My résumé was not on his desk, nor did he bother to ask a blessed question about my theatre background. Instead, he began telling me that he'd "have to jump through hoops" to use me because I didn't have an MFA. I tried to squeeze a word in about my theatre experience in the field and my BFA from one of the best theatre programs in the country.

"So you're like a lot of people!" he jocularly barked. "I mean sure, occasionally, we hire people that don't have a terminal degree, but they're much more ahead of you in the field, like F. Murray Abraham. But he has an Academy Award. Do *you* have an Academy Award?"

About a month later, I submitted a one-act play, *A Question of Ethics*, to Theatre-Studio Inc.

A Question of Ethics centers around two brothers, Joe and Jim Romano. The brothers have arranged a meeting with the Public Speaking lecturer of their younger sister, Katherine. The spring semester has ended, and Katherine has earned a D in the course. The D grade costs Katherine the earned credit hours, which imperils her eligibility for the Tuition Assistance Program. The two brothers meet with Instructor Fortunatto with the intention of persuading him to raise Katherine's grade to a C. If Instructor Fortunatto does not comply to their wish, they plan on offering him a year's worth of free steaks and a luxurious vacation abroad. Instructor Fortunatto listens to the brothers' request and considers it. Then he points out that Katherine has committed a blatant act of plagiarism and that he has no choice but to inform the dean of students, which he will not do if the brothers comply to *his* request.

"What's that?" asks the older brother, Joe.

"I'm asking your permission to court Katherine," Fortunatto responds.

Fortunatto continues by telling the brothers that if Katherine is interested in dating him, he'll raise Katherine's grade to a C. But if the brothers will not facilitate and encourage a courtship with Katherine, Fortunatto will alert the dean of students of Katherine's plagiarism.

I asked another adjunct at Tobit with a theater background to direct. I was to play the part of Instructor Paul Fortunatto.

One mid-October morning, I took the number 4 train to 125th Street. Then I switched to the number 6 local. After a few minutes, the number 6 emerged from the tunnel and continued its run along the elevated track. I was now in the Bronx. I looked out the train's windows; there was little pleasing to the eye. There was usually a fifteen-minute stretch when the train would crawl. Then I finally reached my stop at Westchester Square. I walked downstairs and waited for a privately owned shuttle van. I used to patronize a now-vanishing no-frills diner where I could consume a satisfying if greasy meal for under ten dollars. But this establishment had since closed because its section of Westchester Avenue came under construction.

So I waited. When the shuttle van arrived, it was cramped, and my knees hugged my navel while I sat. During the fifteen-minute ride, the shuttle's door could likely open to the healing or ailing because I would soon be arriving at Hutchinson Metro Center, a complex of healthcare facilities. The very last stop was 1200 Waters Street, Mercy College's Bronx campus. Of course, this was more a site than a traditional campus. But its facilities were high-grade and well maintained, with plenty of sunshine coming through the classroom windows that lightly tinted the hallways' olive-tiled floors. And there was an open-aired atrium.

As I sat there that morning in the fall of 2007, my cell phone rang. I didn't recognize the number.

"Hello."

"Good morning. Am I speaking to Instructor Schwartz?"

"Yes. Good morning."

"Hi. This is Reverend John Gilvey calling from St. Joseph's College."

In addition to being an ordained priest, John had also earned his doctorate in educational theatre. At the time of his initial phone call, John was finishing a biography of Gower Champion. John was a full professor at St. Joseph's Speech and Theatre Department. He planned on taking a leave of absence for the following semester in order to finish his book. He had since published a biography of Jerry Orbach. John Gilvey was an accomplished man. I felt flattered that he thought of me to replace him and take over some of his course load while he took leave. We arranged an interview.

St. Joseph's College is in Brooklyn's Clinton Hill section, a residential neighborhood of quiet avenues intersected by tree-lined streets with prewar brownstones. John Gilvey's office was tucked in the rear of the main building. The usual questions were asked that inquired of my classroom approach and a little about my teaching philosophy. And my résumé was on John's desk. A few days after my interview, John phoned me and said that the next step involved a short and very informal interview with Sister Mary, the dean of the School of Liberal Arts.

What's next? I thought. *A bishop?*

Sister Mary was not wearing her nun's habit, nor did the clergymen don the traditional church vestment. St. Joseph's is a religious college only in name, and I felt more comfortable in my interview with a sister than I did with a rabbi. I was hired to teach one section of Oral Communications and one section of Intercultural Communications.

By late fall of 2007, *A Question of Ethics* had moved from its original space on East Twenty-Fourth Street to the more established and sleeker 78th Street Theater Lab. John Gilvey attended a performance. The audience enters the 78th Street Theatre Lab space through a black-curtained entryway in the back of the house. This was from where I made my entrance. On the night John Gilvey planned to attend, I knew my mother would attend as well. In keeping with my usual preshow peek, around two minutes before the play began, I parted the entryway's black curtain just enough to glean the size of the house. No matter how high the level of dementia praecox I will ever fall victim to, I will never forget the sight of Reverend John Gilvey chatting with my Jewish mother.

By spring of 2008, I was teaching two courses at St. Joseph's, two courses at Tobit, a Mass Media / Media Communications course at the Harlem Rosa Parks Campus of the College of New Rochelle, and the Language of Film at Mercy College's Dobbs Ferry Campus. Add to this a continued staging of *A Question of Ethics*.

I can't look back on my semester at St. Joseph's as particularly rewarding or with much professional pride. My instruction in my Oral Communications class was rote and therefore dull. The content for my Intercultural Communications class was prescriptive and dictated by a syllabus given to me by Reverend Gilvey.

The term *intercultural communications* can take on a number of meanings. To give it a starting point of comprehensive usage, let's say it implies communication between two different cultures. This can mean a pampered middle-aged suburban Jewish American princess hobnobbing with her Dominican hairstylist. Or it could mean a French gay choreographer from Nice making small talk in

English to a working-class Brit lorry driver in a run-of-the-mill pub in London's White Chapel. The directions one can take in teaching the Intercultural Communications course and the amount of potentially unanswerable questions are endless. There's no telling what an imaginative and unorthodox instructor can do.

What I enjoyed most about teaching at St. Joseph's was having the use of Reverend Gilvey's private office. It was a small yet smartly furnished space. From behind his desk, I looked out a large window at the scene on Clinton Avenue. I had high-speed internet. At home, I didn't. There were many a late afternoon when I'd read by the soft pool of light emanating from Gilvey's chrome-plated desk lamp to the sounds of Lizst or Beethoven wafting through the computer. I could have genuinely refined my craft while teaching at St. Joseph's. It was a lovely environment with nice facilities and a supportive administration. But making use of a private office and glutting my brain with YouTube seemed more important at the time.

The Harlem Rosa Parks campus of the College of New Rochelle occupied one floor of a building that leased space to the Studio Museum of Harlem at 125th Street, west of Lenox Avenue. This was my west Harlem debut, having already been on the boards at Tobit's Taino Towers in east Harlem. The Rosa Parks campus was your usual municipal facility for higher learning. The drab environment rivaled Tobit's. The students, faculty, and most of the administration were Black. When I interviewed a good six weeks before the semester began, I was excited. It was an interesting location. West Harlem had long been on the way to gentrification. After a first interview with a senior administrator, I was interviewed by the site director. The senior administrator sat behind me. The site director was a serious woman in her mid-sixties. She had the most interesting office I'd ever been in. I was taken with the African art—mounted masks decrying the most understated of emotions, statuettes ranging from crouching elderly women in prayer to muscular bare-chested warriors complete with shield and spear, statuettes of children with arms aloft as if they were hugging the heavens, and framed oils depicting foaming shores and rustic villages, some lit by sun and some by moonlight. The site director was polite and asked me the usual pedestrian questions about my experience. It was the last time I had any contact with her.

My class and overall experience at CNR's Harlem Rosa Parks site were thoroughly unpleasant. My wages were insultingly low. Chronic lateness, absenteeism, late submissions of homework assignments were the norm. Most of the students were women. Not a few seemed quite troubled and preoccupied with personal problems that were beyond their control. When I administered my midterm, the students finished within an hour, except one. While she worked, I sat behind my desk and read a newspaper. I granted two hours to complete the exam. After an hour and a half, I rose from my desk to stretch my legs. I just walked around the room with arms crossed, looking at the floor.

Then I heard her voice: "Will you sit down? You're making me nervous!"

Thank goodness I was only blocks away from the famous Sylvia's. Many an evening after class, I strolled over and supped on fried pork chops, Southern fried chicken, short ribs, and other life-affirming fare. And I'd always ask my server to put my uneaten corn bread in a to-go container so I could reheat it for breakfast the following morning.

My Language of Film class at Mercy College's Dobbs Ferry campus went hot and cold but certainly had its moments. On the first day of class, we collectively constructed a list of film genres. Under certain genres, I added subgenres. The gangster genre could spill over to the gangster comedy. Or the thriller could spill over to the psychological thriller or action thriller. I concluded the list with schlock, a synonym of trash but a more amusing word to hear and sonorous word to say.

"You can see some C-grade horror films, and you're watching the purest schlock," I said.

I explained that there were romance schlock, epic schlock, prison schlock, biker schlock, and of course, youth schlock, like those embarrassingly stale beach party movies of the early sixties with their campy innocence and Kraft cheese eroticism. I discussed sci-fi/horror schlock, like Ed Wood's *Plan 9 from Outer Space*. This was the first film I screened. Instead of beginning the course with the masters, I began with a quack hack whose films had achieved a cult following for their bumbling ineptitude.

I was very happy that *Plan 9 from Outer Space* got its share of laughs from the class. Within ten minutes of the opening credits, the students recognized the amusingly inferior quality of the acting, script, framing, editing, and overall production values. The biggest laugh came at a somewhat unexpected but understandable moment. While a detective considers his clues to a string of murders, he scratches his jaw with the muzzle of his gun. I reasoned that the students would learn and appreciate higher standards of filmmaking if I began with an untalented amateur. By the time I screened Chaplin's *The Great Dictator*, the students were well versed in such cinematic terms as the *slow pan*, *crane shot*, *medium close-up*, *dissolve*, *cross-cutting*, *intercutting*, and the like.

It was during the very first sequence of *The Great Dictator* when I gave the students a fresh taste of symbolism through the use and positioning of objects. The opening sequence takes place on the WWI battlefield near the Western Front. Chillingly capturing the infantry's blind offensive and its men scurrying in trenches, the camera slowly pans to the right. It stops at Germany's howitzer, otherwise known as Big Bertha, its barrel aimed at the sky at a forty-five-degree angle.

"Does that remind you of a part of the male anatomy?" I rhetorically asked.

That same spring, I rebooted *A Question of Ethics* with a new actor playing the role of Jim. He was a student of mine in my Interpersonal Communications class at Tobit's midtown site. He taught middle school. I think he was accruing more college credits for promotion or an increase in salary. I liked him right away. He was articulate and listened intently to other peoples' opinions before opining himself during discussions. When I found out that he was interested in theatre, I asked him if he had any acting experience. "Some," he said. I read him for the part one night after class, and I cast him on the spot. He was a quick learner and responded well to direction. It was the second time I cast a student of mine in one of my productions.

For the summer of 2008, I taught a couple of night courses at Mercy College's Bronx campus and a few hours of ESL on Monday–Friday mornings for a San Francisco-based company. Classes were held on the campus of Stevens Institute of Technology in Hoboken, the same grounds that Brando and Kazan trod upon while filming *On the Waterfront*.

When Paul Trent over at Mercy informed me that he had a course for me called the Hollywood Western, it was the first time the course had been offered. I had to find a usable textbook and design a syllabus.

Finding a textbook turned out to be problematic. Finding a serviceable text exploring different elements of film aesthetics along with the filmmaking process was simple, but finding a textbook exclusively devoted to a single genre was more difficult. I found studies on the American musical, film noir, the mystery, the silent film, the gangster film, the action film, the war film. I even found one on the biker film. No Hollywood Western. Then I changed my key words to *The Western*. Still no results—unless I was looking for a cheap hotel room or how to cook an omelet. Then I changed my key words to *the American Western*. I found a study of the same title on Amazon. I had it delivered overnight. *The American Western* was penned by a Stephen McVeigh, a Welsh scholar who lectured in the Department of American Studies at Swansea University.

It was about a quarter of the way through Professor McVeigh's study that I began to appreciate his nuanced research of American history. I also came to realize that it was the wrong book for the class. Professor McVeigh's purpose was to weave a construct on the underpinnings, dynamics, contradictions, hypocrisies, and injustices in America's history while using the Hollywood Western as metaphor. A noble ambition. I championed his efforts. But it was cinematic theory. What I wanted was a straightforward survey dissecting the basic elements inherent in the genre. I wanted a chapter on the saloon whore with the heart of gold who tried to steer the outlaw to a conventional life. I wanted a chapter called "Stallions, Colts, Steeds, and Mares," decrying the spiritual importance of a frontiersman's horse. I could have used chapters on different firearms or cowboy and cowgirl fashion, any kind of examination to popularize the genre's artistic texture for the layman.

I ordered *The American Western* for the students anyway because it was well written and I didn't want to begin fall semester without a text. I was offered the course less than a week before the term started. I thought I'd begin teaching the course in a similar way that I began teaching the Language of Film course. I first screened a Western parody, Mel Brooks's *Blazing Saddles*.

Before the film began, I announced, "As a nice Jewish boy from Brooklyn, I seriously doubt that Mel Brooks ever set foot on the badlands of America's West between the Dakotas and the Canadian border, but as evidenced from the film you're about to see, he surely appreciated, understood, and could certainly laugh out loud at what we call the Hollywood Western."

It was a tough genre to sell, and the course was never offered at Mercy College again.

That same fall, another one of my one-act plays was given a staging at Theatre-Studio Inc. at the 78th Street Theatre Lab. *Hot Dogs & Cracker Jacks* centers on a noted British actor filming on location in Brooklyn. In the film, he is to portray a Brooklynite. In order to authenticate his Brooklyn dialect, he visits a local diner in Bensonhurst.

My play *Introductions* was accepted for production to the Strawberry One-Act Festival for the summer of 2009. I staged it at Theatre at St. Clement's Church on West Forty-Sixth Street. The Strawberry One-Act Festival was a competition with a first round, a semifinal, and a final round. Votes were cast by audience members. You could vote for best play of the evening, best director, best actor, and best actress. *Introductions* explores the initial encounter between two female freshman college roommates. One of them is a self-proclaimed gold digger with the aim of landing a husband who is an up-and-coming attorney in the university's third-year law school class. The other roommate is the daughter of former flower children. She loves philosophy because it's "about nothing in particular."

Introductions failed to advance to the semifinals but played in Wild Night. Wild Night consisted of three or four plays that weren't voted into the next round per se but were deemed worthy enough to advance by Strawberry One-Act Festival's artistic director, Van Dirk Fisher, with whom I was to have quite a satisfying association in future years.

Sometime in the past, I'd sent my résumé and a cover letter to the chair of the Borough of Manhattan Community College's Speech and Theatre Department. BMCC was part of CUNY. Its main building was on Chambers Street in Tribeca. In August 2009, I got a call from BMCC's Speech and Theatre Department's secretary. I was to come in and interview for available adjunct positions. The semester would begin in a week.

I was sitting in a room with several other applicants. The chair, an earthy honey-blond late middle-aged Englishwoman, asked each of us when we would be available to teach and how many courses we'd like. I pinched myself to make sure I was not dreaming. Recall that I was paid highest at CUNY and that I'd been out of the system for almost two years. I left the main building with three courses under my belt. The course was my ole bread and butter, Fundamentals of Speech. The classes would meet back-to-back twice a week in rented space in a municipal high-rise building in west Harlem, where I'd seen action not long before.

When I signed my appointment form, I noticed my salary was lower than the rate I'd received from my last CUNY gig. I was paid the same rate as if it were my first semester at CUNY. It had been almost twenty years since I entered CUNY's pearly gates. Adjuncts at CUNY were entitled to an increase in compensation as they continued to teach for the system. I taught at KCC for ten years and multiple semesters at other CUNY schools.

A freckled and carrot-topped gentleman over in payroll agreed that I was entitled to a higher wage. It was only four paychecks into the semester that my higher wage finally kicked in, and it was much higher than I expected. I spoke with a payroll official to ask how my new wage had been calculated. I had difficulty understanding because her explanation lacked a basic coherence and she spoke with a heavy Asian accent. After sitting with her for ten minutes and trying my best to understand, I nodded, smiled, and thanked her. My fourth check of the semester, what with retro pay, had the highest net I'd ever seen. With my three courses at BMCC, two at Mercy, and one at Tobit, I had the highest cash flow in my life. But in the eyes of millions of Americans, I was still living on peanuts and struggling. Yet in the eyes of even more worldwide, I was living like a king.

As the year 2010 began, I was back at the Strawberry One-Act Festival. My play *No Applause Please* focuses on the arrest of a suspect accused of drunken and disorderly conduct in a swank Soho eatery. The suspect is a once-respected actor whose reputation and early promise have since fallen due to his overindulgence in drink and drugs. While waiting to be arraigned, our celebrity suspect is placed in a separate holding area monitored by an officer. It's discovered that the attendant officer has dreams of going on the stage. Our celebrity suspect tries to dissuade the officer from pursuing his dream, goading him on to pursue undercover work wherein *genuine* drama takes place amid *real* life-and-death situations. I played the part of the suspect.

Later that semester, over at Tobit, Herb Wikum called his usual faculty meeting of the Speech Communications Department. These meetings were held in classrooms. No refreshments were served, and attendees were not paid.

I despised Herb's meetings. Herb prattled on about grading policy, attendance records, what we should and shouldn't be doing in the classroom, what we should and shouldn't be telling our students. Then he went on and on about enrollment issues and bookstore problems—an endless mumbo-jumbo of the most mundane, blood-clotting, bureaucratic drivel one could bear to listen to. It was like taking a valium but without the pleasurable relaxation. I failed to see the need for these meetings. He could have easily e-mailed us the information. It was one thing to attend a meeting because of new and improved software to help us keep records or assimilate to a new computer system or if the department you were teaching for underwent a huge shift in policy. Or a departmental meeting could be held for faculty to pool their teaching methods.

These meetings had little to do with teaching. We were told how we needed to be social workers as well as college instructors, always keeping in mind the chaotic lives our students had. What made these meetings more maddening was the sad fact that, in addition to our ridiculously low wage, I could not remember when Tobit's adjunct faculty received a raise. Administration wanted great work, loyalty, and dedication for insultingly low pay. Why was the administration continuing to make the same mistakes, like not submitting the adjunct's letter of appointment on time so she could make the semester's first payroll cycle?

I was forced to hold a class amid the fumes of McDonald's version of beef. There was no one making sure that the bookstores were ordering the textbooks in a timely manner. Management continued making the same mistakes while we needed to improve and self-monitor our performance. Had the management never heard of the adage "You get what you pay for"? If they could respect us for the professional educators we were and pay us an adequate wage for the city we lived in, they'd get new and perhaps improved job performance. I was not going to attend any Faculty Development Day where deli-made hoagies and warm soda were served while my salary remained frozen.

It was in that fateful faculty meeting in 2010 that I communicated the above sentiments to Herb. I did so in an even-tempered tone of voice. I tried my best to convey a "them versus us" attitude as opposed to casting blame on any one individual. I left personalities out of it. Herb was just the messenger. There were about twelve faculty members at the meeting. One of them, Ralph Leventhal, took a shine to my firebrand theatrics. Ralph was an attorney by trade and switched to academia. He was a full-time faculty member in the Business and Liberal Arts Program at Queens College. There was no doubt that Ralph was in a much better financial position than I, what with full-time status at a senior CUNY institution and supplemental income from adjunct work at Tobit. As a fellow Jew, maybe Ralph liked my posturing radicalism toward management. Or maybe he simply admired me for speaking my mind, something seldom done at faculty meetings—or at least the ones I'd attended. Whatever the reason, Ralph referred me to Barbara Green, the director of BALA at Queens College.

There was an opening for an adjunct. When I called Barbara to discuss the possibility of joining BALA's adjunct faculty, she came across as fiercely self-important. She informed me that she would never contact someone cold from a file filled with résumés; she only hired from the inside.

For spring semester 2010, I was reappointed at BMCC but, this time, for only two courses that met back-to-back on Saturdays for three hours each. Classes were held at Lehman College up in the Bronx. Lehman was another senior college in the CUNY system.

My commute up to Lehman was long enough but was easier compared to others I had and others to come. I took the number 4 train up to Kingsbridge Avenue, then walked a block under the roar of the elevated 4 to the campus. This was an actual campus like Brooklyn College and Hofstra University and Mercy College up at Dobbs Ferry. My classes were small. Most of the students worked full-time during the week. I was quite relaxed teaching these classes. The campus was quiet. From inside the classroom, you could hear birds and see open sky.

About midway through the semester, I was observed by a full-timer at BMCC. She had dark curly hair, a svelte figure, and stood around five feet, three inches. She was darkly attractive, an exotic Asian mix. She could have been an odd olio of South American and Indian. She had a tiny tattoo at the base of her spine. She gave me a stellar evaluation, my best to date. She referred me to the department chair for consideration of a full-time position. My observer would soon depart BMCC and travel to Europe for some postdoctoral work.

In addition to being a scholar, she was a matron of the arts. One night, she rented a space in Chelsea and organized what you'd call a public salon. It showcased musicians, storytellers, and balladeers. Soon after our post-observation meeting, I filled out an online application for the full-time position and submitted it to the deputy chair. I wasn't even called in for an interview and failed to secure a reappointment for the following fall semester.

On the fall of 2010, I started teaching one section of the Professional Speech course for BALA at Queens College—CUNY while continuing at Mercy and Tobit.

Queens College's campus is in Flushing. To get there, I took the E train to the Forest Hills stop, then transferred for a city bus. It was about an hour and ten minutes from door to door. The bus dropped me in front of a campus parking lot. From there, I walked around fifty yards to a small building. I opened the door to a carpeted hallway.

On my first morning of class, Barbara met me in the hallway and said, "Hello, Larry. Don't you look nice this morning."

I was dressed for the occasion in a tweed coat, khakis, buttoned-down shirt, tie, and shined loafers over argyle socks. I was not sure whether Barbara took herself or her position too seriously. She had an open-door policy if you needed to talk to her. On three occasions, she walked into my class in the middle of a lecture, completely unannounced and unexpected. She walked in with crossed arms, her jaw clenched like in a vice. She immediately caught my attention. Then some of my students turned around to see what I was looking at. Then she looked over the class and then at me, nodded, and left the class. I wondered what earthly reason she had for doing this.

Then there was the time I went to her office with a question about attendance policy. In a chair at the corner of the room sat a fully clothed male mannequin. When I asked her about it, she told me she put it into the passenger seat of her car when she drove into Flushing from Long Island. I fail to remember the reason she gave, but I knew at that point that she was an odd duck. She was a mature woman but not someone you'd call an "old woman" if you passed her on the street. She had grandchildren. Maybe she lovingly bounced them on her knee while whispering gibberish into their ears, but around BALA, she was like a controlling Jewish mother with a Napoleonic complex.

One morning, I sat behind my desk, sipping coffee in my classroom a few minutes after dismissal.

Barbara came in, crooked her index finger, and said, "I'd like to see you in my office."

I hurriedly obliged.

"I understand that you mentioned *Playboy* in your class."

"Well, actually, I mentioned the *Playboy* magazine."

"Can you tell me your purpose behind this?"

"Well, we were talking about the magazine business in the fifties. Then we started talking about target audiences and how *Esquire*—"

"Well, it's not important that I hear any more of your reasons. I prefer that you don't mention *Playboy* anymore."

"You're the boss," I said. "Is there anything else I shouldn't mention?"

"I can't think of anything at the moment."

"Okay, keep me posted."

I wished her a nice weekend and excused myself.

It was a week before semester's end, and I hadn't heard anything from Barbara about my reappointment for spring. I assumed I was toast because of the unpardonable crime of having mentioned the *Playboy* magazine in class. I decided to call Barbara anyway.

"Hello, Larry."

"I was just wondering about reappointment for the spring."

"Yes?"

"Will I be reappointed?"

"Yes."

I was assigned the same course on the same day in the same time slot. The semester progressed without incident, and I finally capitalized on the knowledge that my BALA students were my best yet. I knew I was teaching future physicians, attorneys, financiers— perhaps even junior statesman. Queens College rivaled Hunter as the most competitive senior college in the CUNY system. BALA was an honors program, so I set high standards. And my standards were usually met.

In March, I was back at the Strawberry One-Act Festival, direct-ing my play *Standing on Ceremony*. It centers on a particularly brutal schoolyard bullying of a an eleven-year-old boy named Bryce. Bryce's arms and shoulders are used as punching bags by a group of his peers. He's severely bruised. When a school official informs Bryce's mother, she visits the family priest for counsel. When the priest hears of the news in his rectory, he suggests that Bryce come along with him and some other boys on a weekend hiking retreat in the Hudson Valley. One of the skills the priest promises to teach the boys is the art of self-defense.

Bryce's mother likes this idea. She returns home and informs Bruce, her husband. Bruce likes the idea as well. But Bryce's maternal aunt, Denny, strongly protests, secretly fearing that, for this weekend retreat, the priest has some hidden designs for the boys. As Aunt Denny is a young graduate student in philosophy at Columbia University, an avowed atheist, punk rocker, and lesbian, her protests fall on deaf ears.

Standing on Ceremony advanced to the final round. Weeks prior to its opening, I posted a flyer on one of the bulletin boards at BALA, in view of all faculty and students to see. Not a word.

Toward the end of the semester, I noticed a young Black woman milling about BALA and spending time talking with Barbara in her office. She turned out to be the faculty member I replaced. She'd be returning in the fall, and I wouldn't.

"We move around adjuncts like chess pieces," Barbara told me.

I always thought Barbara was terribly misguided in her glib assessment of the placing of adjuncts. I've never been a chess player, but what I understand is that when a chess piece is moved, it's done with the utmost forethought, moved with a watchful eye to countermovement and to how that countermovement will in turn change stratagem. A move is made with care. Adjuncts are hardly like chess pieces. They're more like exes and circles, floating aloft in some kind occupational twilight only to land headfirst in an empty square on a tic-tac-toe grid.

In late spring of 2011, I received a message from Van Dirk Fisher over at SOAF that a playwright was looking for a director for his one-act play *With the Assistance of Queen Anne*. I was hired. The play brought a successful novelist and his protégé together for the purpose of gathering information for the novelist's next project, a biography of Queen Anne of Great Britain. As the play progresses, there's an implication that Queen Anne may have harbored lesbian tendencies.

At the same time, there is a growing but repressed sexual attraction between the novelist and his protégé. This effort would mark the second time I'd be paid to direct but the first time I'd be paid in New York City's theater community. The money I made rivaled the price of a four-course meal with a glass of house wine and coffee at one of Manhattan's premier steakhouses.

There's a far cry between history repeating itself and the whimsical predictability of a personal fate.

Less than a week before the fall 2011 semester began, I received a call from a Beatrice Brathwaite, full-time professor in the Mass Communications Department at Medgar Evers College of the City University of New York. We interviewed the next day. Professor Brathwaite had a close-cropped coil and wore horn-rimmed glasses and hoop earrings.

"So one of the many things you can teach them is how to write an outline for a speech, which they'll love you for," Beatrice said when I met her for the first time.

Beatrice was a soft-spoken gentlewoman. I was offered three sections of the Speech Communications course. They were held on Tuesdays and Thursdays and met back-to-back. The classes had twenty-plus students, and the kids were raucous and hard to manage. Most of them were right out of high school. Early on, a Latino affectionately addressed me as bro. I should have taken a sterner approach to this group. The reason I was hired so late was due to an unexpected leave of absence by one of the full-timers so she could have her baby. This very same full-timer turned out to be a former full-timer at Long Island University. She observed me there and gave me a very good evaluation. When the semester began at Medgar Evers, I had some e-mail correspondence with her and downloaded some of her handouts. As the semester progressed, I eased into my own style and methods and ruled with a sterner hand.

The commute to Medgar Evers was a breeze. I took the number 2 or 3 train into Brooklyn and got off at Eastern Parkway. Eastern Parkway had a divider lined with trees and benches. There was plenty of air space to hear yourself think. From the Eastern Parkway station, it was two city blocks to Bedford Avenue, where I turned right. A little way down Bedford Avenue began the typical chain of institutional buildings that comprised a municipal college campus. Most of the academic departments were in the main building, along with the library, administrative offices, and classrooms. Tucked behind the College of Liberal Arts wing was the shared adjunct office.

This was not unusual, yet for the first time in my twenty-two-year career, I felt warmth. I felt warmth from the security guards to the librarians, from the junior administrators to department secretaries. But there was a special warmth and congeniality that came from my fellow adjuncts. Our shared office served as space for multiple departments. There were smiles and laughter, small talk, shop talk, some lighthearted political bantering, and plenty of good-natured ribbing of management. People were on first-name basis.

I remember Walter from the English Department, who laughed out loud at my comments about the Department of Labor. And I remember Margaret, also from the English Department. Knowing Margaret was uniquely sweet because she was a former student of mine from my Brooklyn College days. She told me that, after taking my course, she conquered her fear of public speaking. I came to know adjuncts who taught sociology, psychology, history. Within an hour, I could chat with someone about Freud and Flappers.

The office was small. It merely consisted of ten-by-ten floor space, wedged by two rows of not more than four cubicles to work on a desktop. Yet the office never seemed crowded, and you seldom had to wait for a computer. On the rare occasions you did have to wait, you'd be noticed, and the user would say, "I won't be much longer," sometimes followed by another user who'd say, "Take your time. I'm leaving now."

Dr. Clinton Crawford ran the department faculty meetings. Clinton chaired the Department of Mass Communications. Clinton's field of discipline was African art. By the sound of his accent, I believed he hailed from one of the Caribbean Islands. Clinton spoke to you with both authority and humanity. His meetings were short and sweet, to the point. Clinton didn't smile much. One late afternoon, I was walking down Bedford Avenue toward the main building just after my last class of the day. Clinton was standing outside the building, talking to another gentleman. As I neared, Clinton spotted me, stopped himself in midsentence, and beamed. I could never guess why. I walked with a sense of purpose and wore an expression of self-possession.

At one of our departmental faculty meetings, there were two high-level MEC academic officials. They were Black. Just before the meeting concluded, the two high-level academic officials went to the front of the meeting hall and announced that a special vote would now be taken regarding a sensitive policy at MEC. Only certain faculty members could vote. I was sitting in the front of the meeting hall.

Before the voting began, one of the Black high-level academic officials looked at me and said, "Could you sit in the back of the room?"

Something new fell into my lap for the fall semester of 2011. I get a call from a Dr. Bohr, political science professor for the History Department in the New York School of Applied Sciences Division at Tobit College. Up until that point, I had only taught for Herb in the College of Liberal Arts. NYSCAS offered several survey courses in the arts. One of them was Introduction to Theatre. I was offered a section. The course met once a week at Tobit's Flushing Hills site in Queens, not far from my former haunt at Queens College. I supposed but never confirmed that Dr. Bohr conferred with Herb about filling an opening with someone who had genuine experience in theatre and my name came up. It only took twenty-two years, but I finally had a course in my field of discipline. I could have waited.

Mind that this was a course given as an elective to students who needed to round out their schedules that would satisfy credit requirements. They knew close to nothing about theatre. They knew what actors were. They knew that Broadway was in the Times Square District in the borough of Manhattan. The one current Broadway show they could name was *The Lion King*. None of them knew what a scenic designer was nor what a choreographer did. None of them had ever seen a Broadway play. One of them had read *Death of a*

Salesman. All of them had heard of *Romeo and Juliet,* but no one had read it or discussed it in a class.

When I asked the class if anyone could recall attending a live performance, one young woman said she recently attended her nephew's spelling bee. Another young woman said she saw her cousin play the bassoon in the school's band concert. I stopped asking questions, realizing that they were interpreting my words as if I were speaking Urdu. They'd probably have more interest and could relate more to quantum physics than theatre. Not only did they know close to nothing about theatre or dramatic literature, but they also expected the course to require little to no effort.

When I reviewed the syllabus and noted the few assignments, some of them looked as if they were being thrown naked to Caesar's starving lions. There were two quizzes, a five-page essay on a topic of their choice related to theatre, the reading of two plays, and a traditional midterm and final. When I proposed that we all attend a Broadway play at a discounted rate, they looked like a group of vegans offered ham hocks. I was even stupid enough to assign *Lysistrata* and *Othello* for play readings. I knew that reading a classical Greek comedy was a chore for this group. I could have quizzed them on it, but what good would that have done?

If I wanted to encourage their interest in theatre and drama, I needed a different approach. You might say that I had little respect for the students' concentration and discipline in so compromising my methods and expectations. You could say that I hadn't enough confidence in their literary skills to get through a comedy by Aristophanes or Shakespearean tragedy. You could be right. But remember that these were Tobit College students taking Introduction to Theatre as an elective to round out their schedules and earn the necessary credit in order to satisfy the amount of credits needed for full-time status. They weren't very interested in theatre. Idealism had no place here, nor did Aristophanes or Shakespeare. Realism would lead the way.

On the second day of class, I started talking about baseball. Then I listed the different tiers the game could be played. I started with Little League, moving to middle school, varsity high school, college, tidewater, Minor League, and concluded with the Major

League. Then I correlated this list to the different tiers of theatre. I began with elementary school and concluded the list with Broadway. I changed *Lysistrata* and *Othello* to Neil Simon's *The Odd Couple* and *Barefoot in the Park*. Both plays had a small number of dramatist personae to remember, were comedic, and possessed straightforward relationships, and they were well-crafted. They'd serve my purposes without boring the students.

I stuck to my original syllabus in discussing the different creative personnel involved in a theatrical production. Regarding the discussion of different genres in dramatic literature, I stayed clear of tragedy. I talked about comedy, farce, and musical theatre. I focused on musicals like *West Side Story, Fiddler on the Roof, Oliver, Guys and Dolls*, and dared to explore Brecht's *The Threepenny Opera* to illustrate that even a musical could focus on the criminal underworld. I screened clips of these musicals from YouTube. As for sneaking in some Shakespeare, I indulged myself. I performed Benedick from *Much Ado about Nothing* and Angelo from *Measure for Measure*. I performed the former to convey the fear of love and the latter to convey the sexual corruption of government officials, two problems of the human experiment still alive and well today. I dispensed with the idea of escorting the class to a Broadway play. No problem. The opera awaited.

During the spring semester of 2012, I felt like a buoyant bunny hopper following his twitching nose to the scent of freshly grown garden carrots. By then, I had my regular two Oral Communications courses at Mercy College's Dobbs Ferry campus. The classes met on Fridays. I awoke at 6:00 a.m. to make a 7:20 train out of Grand Central to make an 8:30 class. The second class directly followed. I was reappointed at Medgar Evers for three courses. Herb had informed me before the semester began that there was suddenly a huge cutback in course offerings in Tobit's Speech Department and apologized because he had nothing to offer me.

I saw this coming. I stopped attending faculty meetings, and I long ceased giving Herb the impression that I was grateful for the opportunity to teach at Tobit College. And he resented the fact that

I yearned for better pay and better environments. I did my work and went the distance and cared, but if Herb wanted a raise in my morale, I'd need to see a raise in my paycheck, like any worker.

After thirteen years, Herb and I had a resentful parting of the ways. Good riddance, because Dr. Bohr over at Tobit's NYSCAS offered me a course called the History of Visual Arts. She told me I could teach it like art history and take it in any direction I wanted. I concentrated on painting. I gave lip service to the ancient Greeks, Romans, and Egyptians. I spent a few weeks on the Medieval period, emphasizing that if these theocrats loved their saints so much, they'd allow their artists to paint them as living and breathing human beings, warts and all.

I showed Caravaggio's *Saint Matthew and the Angel* and said, "Look at the crinkled brow and wrinkled forehead of dear Matthew. Here's a saint that's hard at work."

A young woman said, "Yeah, you right."

I found it much easier turning students on to art as opposed to theatre.

It was how the instructor described the work at hand that could be of even more importance than the actual image. When I reached Expressionism, the first image I displayed was Munch's *The Scream*.

I introduced it by proclaiming, "This is what most of the work-force feels like on Monday mornings before their first cup of coffee." I had a field day with Otto Dix and George Grosz. I prefaced my introduction to Expressionism by saying, "The major difference between the Expressionists and the Impressionists is that you can give a six-year-old little girl a Monet or Manet to put on the wall above her bed and it'll more than likely induce sweet dreams. But if you give a six-year-old girl a Dix or a Grosz, it'll likely cause nightmares."

While teaching the History of the Visual Arts, I was homeschooling myself, sometimes all night, while drinking black coffee and munching on brownies. What I gained in weight I gained in knowledge about art history.

Spring 2012 saw the premier of my one-act play *Vengeance Once-Removed* at the Strawberry One-Act Festival. The play explores abuse, single motherhood, and addiction. My next gig at Strawberry came the following summer, directing the one-act *Paula's Visitor*. I got the job like the many others that followed. When plays were accepted for production, the playwrights might have need for a director. Then the artistic director e-mailed directors who had previously worked in the festival. If a director were interested in a play, she'd shoot a cover letter and resume to the playwright.

Paula's Visitor follows a group of American tourists on a safari in Northern Africa. One of the tourists becomes separated from the group. While looking for water, she encounters an ape-like creature who longs for a soul mate. The playwright and I spoke no more than five minutes before he offered me the job. I was paid the same as when I directed *With the Assistance of Queen Anne*. For the role of the ape-like creature, I cast Orlando Rivera, who played the protégé in *With the Assistance of Queen Anne*.

I believe it was Orlando's recommendation that finally secured my next directing gig, the gig that became a turning point, not because it was the most I'd ever been paid to direct, but for purer reasons.

When Dr. Bohr offered me to teach the History of World Music for the fall semester of 2012, I gladly accepted. She knew it wasn't my field of discipline. Introduction to Theatre sections were not running. But I suppose I was receiving favorable teaching evaluations, and after all, both my undergraduate and graduate degrees were in the arts. I had eclectic tastes in music, and it had always been a major part of my life. One of the unsung rewards of bachelorhood is the potential for unbridled cultivation of interests.

I started the class with some obligatory comments on lutes, lyres, the cantata, the mass, and the oratorio. I began the second class by discussing the Baroque period, playing a recording of Pachelbel's Canon.

"If you feel like falling asleep while listening," I said, "feel free. But can you explain to me *why* this induces sleep?"

I think that inspired them to listen. Most of the students grew up on rap, hip-hop, and R&B. I covered Classicism, romanticism, opera, jazz, and a few of its subgenres. I explained how Scott Joplin had a resurgence in the popular American imagination with the release of the 1973 film *The Sting*, with its ragtime score. I covered rock 'n' roll, emphasizing how it couldn't exist without the blues. Then I moved to the British invasion and spent an entire two hours and fifty minutes on the Beatles. I gave a small dose of psychedelic rock. I spoke of disco as much as a musical genre as an agent for socialization and pointed out how utterly silly so many men looked when they tried aping John Travolta's dancing in the film *Saturday Night Fever*. I ended the semester with 1970s punk.

We listened to the Sex Pistols, the Clash, the Buzzcocks, the Ramones. I didn't cover rap or hip-hop. I didn't feel like telling them what they already knew or intellectualizing something they already enjoyed. We learned all the instruments that could comprise a symphony orchestra. My approach to the course was overtly Eurocentric, virtually ignoring the music from the African and Asian continents. Even so, after taking this class, the students knew the Grateful Dead and Brahms's "Isle of the Dead."

Plastic Couch centers on a three-generational Nuyorican family living in Alphabet City in the East Village, Manhattan. Its elder matriarch is suffering from schizophrenia. How does a family coping with daily survival handle mental illness? The play addressed this important question. I met with the young playwright and her brother. *Plastic Couch* would be produced in March 2013 for the Strawberry Play Festival. The plays in the Strawberry Play Festival were short full-length original works that ranged in length from sixty to seventy-five minutes. It seemed that playwright Allisa and her brother were a bit resistant in hiring me.

"I don't think it matters if the director is Latino," I opined. "I think it's more important that the director understand the complexity of family communication amid a crisis." I was asked to submit three references. One of them was from Latino Orlando Rivera, with whom I'd worked twice before. I was sure his reference was the key in securing the position. I asked for $750. My price was accepted.

There were thirteen in the cast. Many of them were new to the business, and a few were making their New York City debuts. Some of the cast had been around for a while and had New York theatre credits but never came close to making a living at it and could hardly be called theatre professionals. The cast was entirely non-Equity. But they were all serious and professional in conduct. The first company read-through was held at the playwright's house in Sunset Park, Queens. We all sat in a lovely lit and adorned living room.

After introductions, I asked the question, "Why is it that family dramas like *Death of a Salesman*, *The Glass Menagerie*, and *Long Day's Journey into Night* still so powerfully speak to us so many years after they were written?"

My answers were lucid and articulate. How I wished I could have received similar answers in my Introduction to Theatre class at Tobit. Slowly but surely, I won over my cast. I never knew until *Plastic Couch* that I possessed the ability to lead. I believe that a true passion and righteous belief in the undertaken enterprise are the two beginning requisites for leadership. I was still a beginning director and still quite wet behind the ears, yet I learned how to gain the respect and trust of actors and inspire them to challenge themselves to bring about their best.

The very same spring, a few weeks after *Plastic Couch* closed, I finally staged a reading of my second full-length play, *A Final Degree*. It's about a troubled adjunct at a community college in Brighton Beach, Brooklyn. Our protagonist meets a new adjunct joining the Department of Communications, and he is immediately smitten. He's in love. Our protagonist's struggle is one for requited love. I thought I'd given this hackneyed theme some fresh and topical treatment, especially since our protagonist is white and his love interest is Black. While staging *A Final Degree*, I taught Introduction to Acting at Medgar Evers. I took an easy approach, doing an extensive physical warm-up, many group improvisations, contemporary monologues, and scene work. I cast one of my female students in a supporting role in *A Final Degree*, and another female student read the stage directions. I was not happy with the reading.

I've done some revising and sent the first ten pages to many theatre companies. It has merited some interest from the likes of the Public Theatre in Manhattan, Florida Studio Theatre, and the

Goodman Theatre in Chicago. At the time of this writing, *A Final Degree* has yet to be produced, but hope remains.

For the fall semester of 2013, Dr. Bohr at Tobit's NYSCAS had originally offered me a course called American Culture. It was dropped from the course catalogue and superseded by Introduction to Opera. I'd been listening to Puccini for years. I'd seen *Turandot* at least twice at the Metropolitan Opera, as well as several productions of *La Boheme*, as well as *Tosca*, and Bizet's *Carmen*. I used *Opera for Dummies* as a textbook. The class consisted of six women and one man. The young man withdrew after the very first class, and an additional two women enrolled. I talked about heroines like Mimi, Tosca, Carmen, Madame Butterfly, and especially Queen Turandot. These women had many devices at their disposal to wrap their men around their fingers, but sometimes the results could be tragic. The students knew I was neither an opera scholar nor a performer because I told them so on the very first day of class. But I did tell them of my theatre experience and how I referenced a couple of operas in a one-act play I wrote. And the ladies knew that when I screened an aria, I was moved.

I screened some Wagner, Mozart, Strauss, and a scene from a little-known English ballad opera, Balfe's "The Bohemian Girl." I added some Gilbert and Sullivan to lighten things up, explaining that just like there was lite beer to give the consumer the same taste as the prototype but not as heavy, so there was also light opera. The ladies enjoyed themselves, and I escorted them to the Metropolitan Opera for a production of *Madame Butterfly*.

For the fall of 2013, Dr. Bohr offered me Introduction to the Arts at a site in Brooklyn I'd never been to. I took the L train all the way to the last stop in Brooklyn. From there, I took a bus to 1344 Pennsylvania Avenue. The bus stopped in front of a parking lot to a shopping plaza. The plaza was configured at a ninety-degree angle. On the plaza's left side, wedged between a Boston Market and a CVS, there stood yet another storefront Tobit College, secure and proud in its ubiquity, like your neighborhood Burger King. My experience teaching Introduction to the Arts was well worth the commute. I was like the proverbial pig in shit, wriggling my toes in the cool mud, my coiled tail atingle.

I chose *Perceiving the Arts: An Introduction to the Humanities* for my chosen text. There was an introductory chapter that expounded on the author's notions on how art could be interpreted and the effect it could have on our lives. He followed this with chapters on painting, printmaking, photography. Then came sculpture, architecture, music, literature, theatre, cinema, dance. I skipped architecture entirely. The examination was rooted in the technical and industrial. It bored me. I had a little more fun with sculpture. I showed many slides of statues from Hellenistic Greece, spoke at length about Michelangelo, both the artist and man, while students looked at his *David*. Then I moved on to Rodin's *The Thinker*. To leave a lasting impression, I concluded with a brief appreciation of African American sculptress Elizabeth Catlet's *Singing Head*. For the other chapters, I basically shared what I loved while following the course objectives.

I screened the original 1968 version of *Planet of the Apes*, claiming that only in democratic republics could a film portraying intelligent and talking apes gain such widespread popularity. When we were sampling the modern masters in painting and arrived at Modigliani, I pointed out the slight resemblance in his portrait of Madame Kissling to The Beatles drummer, Ringo Starr. So when we began covering The Beatles, the students already possessed a heightened perception of drummer Ringo. I compared punk to opera in their fetishizations of the human voice. I gave the students a sample of both the original blues version of "Hound Dog" and Elvis Presley's.

I didn't take a chronological approach. I thought it would be more interesting if I followed Brahms with the Beach Boys, traveled back to Beethoven, and then hurtled forward to the Beatles. For literature, I stayed clear of the high-brow, giving the additional reading of Lorraine Hansberry's *Raisin in the Sun*. How convenient that the title was taken from a Langston Hughes poem, so when we covered some of his wonderful and deeply sympathetic short fiction, his reputation preceded him. I spent two classes on theatre.

When it came to dance, I opened the class demonstrating the five ballet positions. It was an intended struggle for me to properly align my feet for the fourth and fifth positions. "You could almost consider ballet dancers to be professional feet contortionists. And you could always spot ballet dancers on the street because they walk in second position." I proceeded to demonstrate the Grand seconde, the Demi-hauteur, and the Ronde de jambe a terre.

"And if you think I'm now going to dance on point," I said, "you'll believe that I'm one-quarter Cherokee."

I discussed the rigors of ballet training, likening it to a prize fighter's training.

"But when ballet partners make contact," I said, "they don't break bones or pummel flesh like boxers. They ever so gently lift their partners from the waist."

I screened some videos of Nureyev and Baryshnikov. Then I took a complete 180-degree turn and brought up square dancing as an example of folk dance. From hootenanny, I segued to hokum in my introduction to the can-can. The students dug it. I proceeded to the jazz dance and emphasized its African origin. I screened the scene in *Saturday Night Fever* wherein John Travolta's Tony Manero pulled out his bag of tricks in his solo on the disco dance floor. I noted the contrast in his improvisation to the precise choreography called for in ballet. It was probably one of my most successful classes ever on a subject I knew very little about.

I upped my director's fee for my next project at Strawberry One-Act Festival. I now asked for a sum that could pay for *two* multicoursed steak dinners at a prime Manhattan steakhouse. The play was called *9/11/02*. A woman is accused by her son of embezzling money left to his father after losing his life in 9/11. A few days after the final performance, I received a phone call from James Jennings, artistic director of the American Theatre of Actors. James had contacted me several years earlier after I sent him a copy of *A Question of Ethics*. He liked the script and suggested that I send him a full length. This time, he called me because he was looking to expand his pool of directors in residence. He claimed to have seen *9/11/02*. I returned his call, and we arranged to meet in Jim's office.

Jim founded the American Theatre of Actors sometime in the midseventies. It shares the same building with Manhattan Criminal Court at 314 West Fifty-fourth Street. It has three performance spaces: the John Cullum, the Beckman, and the Sargent. After our chat in Jim's office, he showed me around ATA. He explained that ATA's mission was to workshop new plays set in the present and to occasionally stage the classics. Jim made it clear to me that he "couldn't pay anything." I shrugged my shoulders and said okay. Here was an opportunity to direct full lengths at an established theatre company.

After touring ATA, Jim and I returned to his office. He gave me four or five scripts to read. I decided to try my hand at a play called *Tea in a Tempest*. I notified Jim, and he told me he'd contact the playwright in Pennsylvania for permission. Permission was granted.

In *Tea in a Tempest*, an upper-middle class wife gets wind of her husband's philandering with a younger woman. Our cuckolded wife hosts a small gathering at which only tea and biscuits are served. When all the guests have their tea in hand, our hostess toasts to her impending divorce. All are in on the joke except the cheating husband.

Jim gave me the Beckman for a five-performance run. I cast the play from his file of ATA actors and with three actresses with whom I'd previously worked. Rehearsals took place at ATA. Jim attended opening night. As the audience filed out of the theatre after curtain call, I followed to find Jim sitting on a stairwell near the theatre's entrance. He was grinning. I'd found a home to stretch my directing chops.

Not long after *Tea in a Tempest* closed, I went into rehearsals for *The Poisons*, written by my old colleague at CUNY, Richard Helfer. *The Poisons* took place at the kingdom of Versailles during Louis XIV's reign. There's an underground cell in Paris consisting of Satanists, covens, and freelance alchemists determined to poison the king. *The Poisons* was accepted for production at New York's Fringe Festival. I was cast as Gabriel Nicolas de la Reynie, chief of police and general aide-de-camp to King Louis XIV. The play was staged in a large black box in a cultural center on the Lower East Side. It ran for nine performances.

I was slowly but surely carving a modest career in theatre, had twenty-five years of college teaching, held a BFA and MA in theatre, and could scarcely get a nibble for a full-time position in a university theatre department. It wasn't because I was lacking in ability or knowledge. It was because I didn't have the right master's degree. I only had an MA, and you needed an MFA to be seriously considered for a full-time tenure track position in a university theater department that serves undergraduate theatre majors. I even went online, searching for opportunities to teach theatre or acting in correctional institutions. I knew that there was plenty of untapped talent in men and women who were living behind bars. No luck in corrections.

Not long after *The Poisons* closed, I received devastating news. It turned out that speech courses were no longer required for students to earn their degrees at Medgar Evers. This was the result of a new policy enacted by the CUNY chancellor's underlings at CUNY headquarters in Manhattan. The enacted policy was dubbed Pathways. This new policy made it easier for CUNY students to transfer to other institutions. The lesser the required credits, the easier to transfer.

I still do not understand the logic of such a policy. I'd taught at MEC for three years. It was an easy commute. I liked the students. The students liked me. I shared an office with other adjuncts who were warm and friendly. I received good teacher evaluations from the students and good observations from full-time faculty. I was earning a competitive wage and receiving an excellent health-care package. And all these were taken from me like a paper napkin from a dispenser by men who didn't know me or my work. Pathways didn't affect all CUNY schools, just a few of its senior colleges. I already knew that job security wasn't one of CUNY's strong points. But this was outrageous and completely unexpected. Yet Lady Luck would yet again work her charms.

Some ten days before the fall term of 2014 began, I received an e-mail from the chairman of the Humanities Department at yet another CUNY school, New York City College of Technology, better known as City Tech. I already had my schedule from Mercy and Tobit, so I could only manage to take two of the three courses offered. My two Speech Communications classes were back-to-back and met on Tuesday and Thursday afternoons. I took the C train to the Jay Street Metro Tech stop in Brooklyn. This was certainly not one of Brooklyn's garden spots—heavy traffic coupled with over-crowded sidewalks amid crude fast-food eateries, family and criminal court buildings, chain retailers, and a lone pizzeria.

Once I reached City Tech's main building, there were uniformed security guards. Then I scanned my City Tech ID on a turnstile. Oh, the charm of it all! Then I walked through a wide hallway, descended a few stairs, and took my place at the end of a curved waiting line to board one of the elevators. There were times when I'd wait ten minutes before squeezing into one. On many occasions, the elevator reeked of curry, one of my favorite spices.

My classes were a mix of Blacks, Asians, Hispanics, a stray White here and there. The level of students was on par with my Medgar Evers students. There was no shared office space for adjuncts. There was a computer center that called itself a faculty lounge, yet food and beverages were prohibited. During my first week of classes, I saun-tered over to the cafeteria on the fifth floor. The frankfurters were suffering from an under-injection of food dye. The fried chicken cutlets looked like pummeled and deboned turkey wings dipped in liquid bronze. The goulash looked like a mélange the royal family's executive groundskeeper would serve its most prized hunting hound. As for the mushroom barley soup, the bits of barley looked more like chipped baby teeth, and I couldn't find a single mushroom. I braved a cup of coffee. I walked among the student-filled tables. I'd heard the N word uttered many times before at other colleges, but this time, it had a particularly odious effect.

There were no surprises in my classes. But there was one female student who had an absolute pathological fear of public speaking. She wouldn't even try. I used the persuasive skills I taught for so many years to help her. I used selective appeals to her ego. It eventu-ally worked, and she conquered her fear.

Jim Jennings invited me back to direct another full-length play at ATA. I chose a play called *Spoiling for Justice*. A young man reads in the newspaper that a local couple's pet snake has escaped from its cage and attacked and killed the couple's newborn. The young man then leaves his apartment to confront the couple. This time, Jim gave me the Sargent Theatre, two flights up from the Beckman, for a ten-performance run.

Back at City Tech, I was informed by the chairman of the Humanities Department that I'd be observed by a Professor Eileen Fink. For my lesson, I planned to discuss and creatively delineate the early stages for preparing a short informative presentation. I'd done the same lesson many times before while being observed with positive results. I would explore topics. Then with the help of the students, proceed to break the topic down to a doable purpose statement, then break down the purpose statement to a thesis statement. On the day of my observation, I felt secure and confident in my experience.

As always, when I was observed, I dressed in a shirt and tie. I started to take attendance. Professor Fink had yet to arrive. I was reading the last name on my attendance roster when Professor Fink walked into the classroom. We'd never met, but I e-mailed my lesson plan and my desired outcome. She was a tall and thin elderly woman with reddish hair. I can't recall her features because memory won't allow. I carried on with my class. I lectured, and students asked questions. I addressed each student by name, all the while seeking additional questions. I was careful with humor because Professor Fink looked like one of the most miserable people I'd ever seen. She had a notepad on her desk, but I couldn't recall her writing more than a few intermittent words. An active observer would write in sentences. For the most part, she just looked at her notepad and now and then glanced at her watch.

About halfway through the class, I chose to entirely disregard her. After wishing my students a happy weekend, they were dismissed. Fink stayed seated. As the students began filing out the door, I walked over to Fink. She glared at me.

"So when can we meet for our post-observation discussion?" I asked.

"I'll put it in your mailbox, and you can read it."

She didn't open her mouth to utter these words. She snarled them through pouty lips in a voice evocative of a bratty little girl. It had always been custom for my observer and me to sit down to meet after the observation.

I received a scathing evaluation. Besides starting the class on time and speaking in an audible voice, I didn't do one thing right. She claimed my lesson was much too simple for the caliber of the students at City Tech. She claimed I was disorganized and slipshod in my explanation of terms. I have always been open to criticism—if it was constructive and thoughtful. Fink's comments were just generalized and mean-spirited.

I met with the chairman of the Humanities Department. Dr. Lowe was a thirty-something Brit whose field of discipline was linguistics. She had to sign off on my Observation after I'd sign it, which I hadn't done yet. Dr. Lowe had read my observation evaluation, and I explained to her how unfair and inaccurate I thought Fink's comments were. I also told Dr. Lowe that I successfully taught for many years at Hofstra University on Long Island and had always received favorable evaluations.

"Surely you must have heard of Hofstra University," I said.

I was told that I could write a response and that it would be included with my observation evaluation in my file. Write a response, I did. When describing Fink's comments, I used terms like *mean-spirited*, *nasty*, *inaccurate*, *misguided*, and *destructive*. I forgot who told me, but I found out later that Professor Fink gave a bad evaluation to all she observed. Poor woman. This was a deeply troubled creature who had evidently lost her ability to cope with the inevitable problems that came with living. Could it be that I reminded her of someone she despised? Was I a painful reminder that she had not shared a bed with a firm-bodied man since the Carter administration?

But looking back on this incident, I can only feel pity for a person who, in my perception, is in terrible need of a little fun. And to channel your frustration on the defenseless? How utterly sad and sadistic.

Soon after my meeting with Dr. Lowe, I received an e-mail from a staffer at Pathways in Technology Early College High School. PTECH occupies two upper floors in Paul Robeson High School on Albany Avenue in Crown Heights, Brooklyn. It functions in association with the New York City Department of Education, City Tech, and IBM. PTECH is the brainchild of its dreadlocked principal, Raheem Davies. A few courses at PTECH are taught by college instructors commissioned by City Tech. I became one of them. Why Dr. Lowe referred me to PTECH, I will never know. I was expected to teach a Speech Communications course to urban high school students with the same rigor and expectations as I would to college students. PTECH's mission was to provide IBM with a pool of tech-savvy high school graduates for internships. I was appointed two courses for the spring semester of 2015. I'd be paid my regular CUNY wage and retain my health-care package.

On February 2015, I was back on the boards at Strawberry One-Act Festival, directing *Across*, written by Michael Swiskay, with whom I attended Roslyn public schools and with whom I performed in several Royal Crown Player productions, Roslyn High School's after-school drama society. We formed a friendship and remain friends to this very day.

There are high schools in New York City that are quite difficult to teach in. There are high schools with an element that interferes with others' desire to learn. There are high schools where teachers fear for their safety. PTECH was absolutely none of the above. It had a very small student body comprised of young ladies and gentlemen. As healthy teens, they became a bit boisterous in the hallways but never did any of them say an unkind or disrespectful word to me. But they were still high school students given to collective high school behavior, and PTECH was still a high school. Several uniformed NYPD officers scanned the students' bags. And students had to walk through a metal detector as well. Thank goodness I was spared this process.

I loathed the environment. My liaison to City Tech was a lovely young woman, and one of the secretaries in the main office could be cordial at times. The other secretary despised me at first sight. And by then, I should have known there were certain student populations who needed sheer drilling and discipline, not the waxing of philosophy or wit. By then, I should have learned that there were many young students who would take advantage of an agreeable presence. If only someone could have told me to become the necessary tyrant in order to achieve results. My first semester at PTECH went well enough. I adjusted as well as I could. In my second and third semesters, things got out of hand, and I started to crumble.

Sometime in May 2015, I met a chap named Lewis Payton at a diner on West Fourteenth Street in Manhattan. We met to discuss the possibility of my directing Lewis's one-act play *The Prophet* for SOAF in the Summer of 2015. *The Prophet* brought together southern barrister Thomas Grey and rebel slave Nat Turner in Nat's cell. Nat is awaiting his hanging, and Grey wishes to wrest Nat's confession for his crimes. Grey seeks a confession that will serve American history, a confession that will preserve the white man's perception of the Black man as unruly savage without the faculty of reason and be treated as such. Nat toys with Grey and, for a while, play-acts the role assigned to him. As a preacher and biblical scholar, Nat tries to absolve Grey of his debauchery and adultery.

The Prophet played at Tato Laviera Theatre on East 123rd Street in the Taino Towers Cultural Building, one of Tobit College's former sites. *The Prophet* advanced to the finals. The final performance was played at the Leonard Nimoy Thalia Theatre at Symphony Space at Broadway and Ninety-Fifth Street. Lewis wrote me a stellar recommendation. It has served me well. There I was, moving from project to project, earning respect from playwrights, actors, producers. This worsened the lying and disrespect that would soon come my way.

PART V

HEADING TOWARD
THE BRIDGE

In the fall semester of 2015, I returned to PTECH.

I began my day looking at NYPD officers in a dreary and drafty front hallway of a public school. I took the elevator to the sixth floor. I passed an encased photograph of former New York governor George Pataki, President Obama, and former New York City mayor Mike Bloomberg. Pataki and Obama smiled and looked relaxed. Bloomberg looked like he was about to be given a hypodermic injection of cod liver oil on his tongue. I retrieved my daily attendance roster from my mailbox in the main office and was given a dirty look from one of the secretaries. Then I walked downstairs, unlocked my classroom door, and waited for a class of eight to arrive.

There was always the same student who was the only one to arrive on time. When he entered the room, he dragged his feet to a student desk and went to sleep. My plea of "Please wake up" was ignored because he was already asleep. He began to snore. Then the rest of the eight male students came in at maybe one or two at a time. They were all wearing T-shirts and sweatpants because they had come from their Physical Education. They're unprepared and asked if it would be all right if they could go to their lockers to get their textbooks.

And I was told to teach this class with the same rigor and expectations that I'd bring to a college level. What a sly con! If I tried to see Principal Davies, he was never in. If I asked the secretaries when he was expected, it was always "He should be in later." My e-mails to him went unreturned.

There was an English teacher who was also appointed through City Tech. When I told her about the situation, she told me, "Don't worry about it. Davies is a con man." I took her word for it. I saw little to contradict her assessment.

At Tobit's Bensonhurst site, I was appointed the class Introduction to Theatre. It was a thirty-minute ride from downtown Manhattan on the D train to Brooklyn. Again, it was a very small class consisting of mostly young Russian women with little to no knowledge of the world of theater. And then there was Veronica. Veronica was Hispanic. She had a generally scraggly appearance— frizzy hair, a case of mild acne lining her cheeks. She always wore faded jeans, a jean jacket, and work boots.

As was my custom on the first day of class and every subsequent class, I told the students to put away their mobile devices. "*Away* means in your bag, your backpack, your coat pocket—anywhere that's completely out of sight."

Veronica would simply ignore my request. She'd always be on her iPhone, occasionally looking up when I'd screen a scene from a play. On the third class of the semester, I decided to do something about it.

After the rest of the students put their iPhones away, I said to Veronica in a very patient and even fatherly tone, "Veronica, the standard for my class is that all iPhones are put away when class begins. Can you do this for me?"

Then she looked at me as if I asked her to perform striptease. Then she began a foul-mouthed diatribe about following my rules and that she wasn't bothering anyone "so what the f—ck difference does it make!"

"Okay," I said, "Then carry on."

With this response, she looked even more hateful than when I made my original request.

There are college instructors who aren't bothered by students on their iPhones. There have been plenty of times when I've walked by classes and witnessed students shamelessly scrolling while their instructors lectured. I won't allow this and will never allow it.

Another instructor would have let Veronica continue along. I decided to consult the site director. On the fourth class, nothing changed. It was likely that the site director did absolutely nothing. I now had the option of appealing to the dean of students at Tobit's Twenty-Third Street site.

To hell with that, I thought. *Why worry so much about it?*

Just imagine how Veronica's hard-working mother and father would feel if they knew Veronica's attitude? They worked so hard to save money for Veronica's tuition so she'd be the first one in her family to attend college. What a waste. This was pure schema on my part, but it helped me.

Veronica failed to attend the next two classes, missing two quizzes. She attended the seventh class and used her iPhone far less than in previous classes. We reviewed for the following week's midterm. Veronica missed the midterm. She had a spotty attendance for the rest of the semester. She barely passed one quiz, failed to submit the one short term paper, and failed the final exam. All in all, she was absent seven times out of fifteen class meetings. When I uploaded my final grades at the end of the semester, I clicked on F when I came to Veronica.

Goodbye and good riddance. Or so I thought.

For spring of 2016, I taught six classes and three different courses at three different sites. There I was in my midfifties with the same leg work and load that I had in my midthirties. I had my usual two classes at Mercy's Dobbs Ferry campus on Fridays, three classes at Pathways to Technology High School in Brooklyn and, another first for me, the History of American Music at Tobit's Forest Hills site. The first song I played was "Frank and Jesse James," the very first track on Warren Zevon's very first LP. It's an ingenious blend of American lore, lyrics, and melody. Then I played Kate Smith's "God Bless America," followed by Woody Guthrie's "This Land," which I learned was a response to Irving Berlin's naïve anthem.

I concentrated on the turn of the nineteenth century to the present. I did a good deal of homework. If I were to play artists like Ella Fitzgerald, Jerome Kern, and Billie Holiday, I wanted to talk about them with a fair amount of authority. I spent a good deal of time discussing and playing various show tunes. I discussed the oh-too-democratic tradition of band coverage and artists covering other artists. I discussed and played the work of some of the more successful film composers like Max Steiner, Miklos Rozsa, Bernard Hermann, Quincy Jones, John Williams, and Jerry Goldsmith.

Sometime in early March, City Tech sent a full-time professor to observe me at PTECH. When I met her in her office at City Tech a few days after the observation, she began by saying, "Well, Laurence, I can certainly say that you are a teacher and should be teaching."

Gee, golly thanks a whole bunch for putting to rest any lingering doubts I might have nursed. Now I can start sleeping peacefully.

It wasn't so much *what* she said than *how* she said it. I naturally brought a somewhat defensive style of listening after my previous City Tech observation with the Wicked Witch of CUNY. I received a good observation, with an especially favorable nod to my interactions with students.

In the early spring, I directed *Perception of Color* at the American Theatre of Actors for a ten-performance run. A young Caucasian man living with a Black woman plans on introducing her to his parents. However, he doesn't want to tell his parents that his girlfriend is Black. He wants it to come as a surprise. His girlfriend has serious doubts about this decision. I directed a cast of four in a beautifully written script that revealed the folly of race identity within both platonic and romantic relationships. A theatre director could often see the fruitful results of his labor—not necessarily so a college instructor, especially with lazy students.

During spring break, I spent five days in Miami Beach. When I returned home, I found a letter in my mailbox from City Tech. It informed me that I was not to be reappointed for the fall. It could have been because I submitted sloppy and poorly kept attendance or grade roster sheets at the end of semesters to the Department of

Humanities. It could have been because of poor teacher evaluations from the students. Or it could have been because my latest observer thought I wasn't right for this kind of position. This was the most valid reason.

I found the school itself to be the usual public institutional chamber of horrors. Surly cops roamed the hallways. The library wasn't even open. There wasn't even a decent eatery in the neighborhood where I could go and have a relaxing lunch during my break. The Wi-Fi was terrible. The IT staffer was always difficult to find if I had a problem with the laptop I used in class to project images against the soiled screen. And the classes were oversized and unmanageable. They were nice kids but wild and restless. I had to constantly raise my voice in order to maintain their focus. There were times I bellowed with uncontrollable anger. Sometimes I'd leave the building with a headache and sore throat. I couldn't ask for a more alien environment.

When I finished reading the letter from City Tech, I closed my eyes and sighed. Like a paroled convict, I was relieved to regain my freedom. I knew I'd lose some significant income and perhaps my health insurance, but at the price of sanity? I did my time.

In June, I e-mailed Dr. Bohr at Tobit, informing her what courses I was interested in teaching for the fall and the times I was available.

Her returned message stated, "I'd rather talk to you about a former student. Can we meet in my office?"

Dr. Bohr said that she understood that I failed a student by the name of Veronica Sanchez in Introduction to Theatre.

"That's right. What about it?"

"Well, she said that she tried to contact you about making up an assignment and rescheduling an exam she missed."

"That's not true."

We went back and forth like this while I maintained that Veronica never contacted me. Something stunk.

"Well, I'll double-check my Tobit e-mails to see if I overlooked any message that Miss Sanchez sent me," I said.

I felt degraded. Then I mentioned courses for the fall. Dr. Bohr waddled over to a desk and started shuffling papers.

"Well, it seems that I'm short on courses. I don't think I can offer you anything."

I'd looked online and found no cut back in course offerings for the fall in the Arts Department. Then Dr. Bohr told me that Herb Wikum told her that I sometimes missed class to go on auditions.

"Untrue," I said. Then I excused myself and told Dr. Bohr I'd be in touch.

Herb Wikum once mentioned in a faculty meeting that he once submitted his final grade roster for a class that included several students who failed. Dean Wish subsequently asked him to pass the students who failed. I wasn't surprised. And it was common knowledge among the faculty ranks that if there was ever a dispute between faculty and a student, administration always took the student's side. There was no end to the lies and hypocrisy at Tobit College.

Fahara Fentil is the actual chairman of the Arts Department at NYSCAS. I met her a couple of times at Arts Department meetings where most of the instructors didn't attend. Fahara seemed like a thoughtful woman. I wrote her an expansive letter detailing my meeting in Dr. Bohr's office and what transpired. I concluded the letter thus:

> I'm confused about something regarding the Arts Dept. at NYSCAS. As you are the chairman, wouldn't that give you final say over class assignments? And wouldn't it therefore mean that you could have told Dr. Bohr to give me a class? How far did you appeal to her on my behalf? Did you use the power of your position? And why is Dr. Bohr of all people assigning the arts courses? Shouldn't you be doing that? My final process of appeal led me to Dean Wish. When I explained to him what happened he asked me if I had a

problem with a student? Regarding my incident with Veronica Sanchez, was that the cause of my non-reappointment? What exactly did I do? Is it out of line for a college instructor to ask students to put away their mobile devices? I've never had a problem with this at the other and better colleges where I've taught. After a few weeks of waiting for the Dean's response, this is what he e-mailed, "Enrollment is down in the History Department, there's nothing I can do for you." I do not teach in the History Department! Can't administration do a blessed thing right? I teach in the Arts Department. Maybe, I'm being very unreasonable and overreacting. Maybe, it's as you told me, wherein the instructors teaching arts courses in NYSCAS should be teaching in their area of discipline. But maybe not. Maybe I've been lied to and disrespected and been blamed for something that I didn't do.

Maybe when all is said and done; Herb Wikum, Dr. Bohr, and Dean Wish deserve one another. It's a shame that after all my years at Tobit, my departure arrives with lies and deceit and pettiness. But, there's plenty more where that comes from at Tobit College. Tobit College is the laughingstock of academia, a decrepit chicken-shack on a boulevard of swank French bistros, a disgrace.

Regrettably,
Laurence

It's a good thing I never sent the letter.
So now I was dealt the double whammy with non-reappointment at both Tobit and City Tech.

Then the summer of 2016 arrived.

I started sending out résumés. I set up an interview at Zoni Language Center, an English Language Academy in Elmhurst, Queens. I'd taught ESL at Zoni during the summer of '04. I left on very good terms. A plump Russian woman interviewed me. When asked how I'd teach past participle, I said I'd compare it to simple present. Zoni must have been desperate. I was offered the position of a substitute teacher. Whenever a full- or part-time instructor couldn't make it to class, I was contacted to step in. Most times, I knew a week in advance. The wage was low. A fast-food worker could almost earn as much flipping burger patties. But I needed the work to rebound. And Zoni was a very pleasant place to work. Most of the students were South American and were very respectful. And they could laugh. In addition to Zoni, I had a Monday evening Mercy class in Manhattan. And thank goodness I was hired to direct two one-acts at SOAF in the summer of 2016, both comedies—*Flight 987* and *The Waitress*. Things would work out.

I started fall 2016 with the lightest course load I can remember—three courses at Mercy College and substituting at Zoni.

Around the third week of September, as I left my apartment to celebrate Rosh Hashanah at my mother's, the phone rang.

"Hello, is this Instructor Laurence Schwartz?"

It was the College of New Rochelle calling. This time it was from the site on Fulton Street in Brooklyn. Two courses suddenly became available, Introduction to the Thriller and English Modes. A full-timer suddenly took sick leave. It was arranged that I'd arrive the very next day for a general interview and a short demo lesson.

The site director was an attractive middle-aged Black woman. We met in her office, and she asked me about my last teaching experience at the College of New Rochelle's Harlem site.

I said it was "quite something."

Instead of probing my answer, she said, "You come highly recommended."

I didn't believe her. Then she told me to go upstairs to room 315, where she would meet me in a few minutes for my demo lesson. There were a few classes in session, and no one was in the hallways. It was a quiet place. That was the only thing I liked about it. I learned later that there were more classes offered in the evening because most of the students worked full-time during the day.

My demo lesson explored the differences between film and theatre. It lasted just under ten minutes. Then the site director said, "That was fine." Then she excused herself and told me, "I'll be back soon to talk further. Nice job."

I was hired. The wages were low—$1,800 for English Modes and $2,100 for Introduction to the Thriller. They both met once a week. Introduction to the Thriller met in the evening and English Modes late morning. Thank the gods that class times didn't conflict with my Mercy schedule.

English Modes was a basic survey course of literature. I was given a syllabus that prescribed the choices of the novel, short fiction, drama, and poetry. I was given a marvelous anthology that included a thoughtful variety of tone, style, and period.

On the first day of class, I began discussing the different styles of poetry. Then I turned to Etheridge Knight's "Hard Rock Returns to Prison from the Hospital for the Criminally Insane." Mr. Knight began writing poetry while doing hard time for robbery.

I said, "Listen to Mr. Knight give a personal eyewitness account to life behind the wall." Then I gave an impassioned recitation. After that, I recited some of Walt Whitman's "Song of Myself," followed by Allen Ginsburg's "A Supermarket in California." For drama, I covered my beloved *Raisin in the Sun*. I covered several short stories and Kate Chopin's novel *The Awakening*, which I thought a ridiculous choice. Its heroine is a bourgeoisie wife and mother wrestling with her restrictive gender roles while she vacations on Grand Isle at a resort on the Gulf of Mexico.

I realized it's an important novel in American fiction that gives voice to the many unspoken yearnings of women, but I found the prose clunky and unmoving. I thought the heroine moved in an entirely different circle and society than the students. Ann Petry's *The*

Street would have been a much better choice. Its heroine is a Black single mother living in post-WWII Harlem and desperately trying to make a life for her son and herself.

The Introduction to the Thriller was a bit of a lark. I had a good deal of trouble with tardiness and absenteeism. Before each class began, I had to alert the on-site security guard for use of the audiovisual equipment. CNR Brooklyn didn't have IT personnel.

Now that my course load was back to normal, I decided to get back to work on my stage directing. I went over to ATA for a few full-length scripts. I chose the drama *Leaving Lannahassee*.

Lannahassee is a backwoods region in Georgia. The play's one set is the front porch to a kind of halfway house where two mentally dim convicts live. Both convicts have committed violent crimes, but they were done from passionate rage and neither convicts had a previous criminal record. The halfway house was founded and is managed by a Miss Mercy, a beer-guzzling religious fanatic. The younger and smarter of the two convicts is approached by a local young woman. She claims that she has been sexually abused by her drunken father. She seduces the young con and convinces him to murder her father so she can inherit his money and leave Lannahassee for the big city. And she promises the young con that she'll take him with her.

During the early stages of rehearsal, I was quite excited about the cast, all except the actor who played the small but quite juicy role of Sheriff Calloway. I'd worked with Steve before in a leading role, and he had trouble memorizing his lines. Sheriff Calloway was a much smaller role, but Steve's memorization problems persisted. When I phoned Steve to tell him I had to replace him, he said, "Okay." He knew exactly why. Playing a redneck sheriff was the freest I'd ever felt on stage. And I reached the age when I could empathize with Sheriff Calloway's frustrations and tap into the genuine love he had for Miss Mercy. The play was well received and got a good review in an online theatre journal.

Sometime in late January, I got a call from Dr. Bohr at Tobit. She offered me an Introduction to the Arts class for the spring. I gladly accepted. This time, I took academic matters into my own hands.

I'd completely dispense with architecture, sculpture, and dance. I'd cover music, theater, literature, painting, and film. And I'd cover Ann Petry's novel *The Street*. For painting, I spent a good deal of time on Expressionism, particularly Otto Dix and George Grosz's grotesque depiction of Weimar debauchery. I screened Tod Browning's *Freaks*. I covered Miguel Pinero's prize-winning play, *Short Eyes*. My musical repertoire included but was not limited to classical, opera, blues, jazz, rock 'n' roll, glam rock, acid rock, punk rock, pop rock, folk, country rock, and a smattering of industrial.

At the College of New Rochelle in Brooklyn, I was reappointed one section of English Modes, and I had my regular two courses at Mercy's Dobbs Ferry campus.

It had been several years since I posted my résumé on Indeed, the job search site. I'd recently narrowed my job alert to theater jobs, both teaching and nonteaching. In mid-March of 2017, I finally received a job alert that raised my eyebrows—the Art of Improvisation at the Summer Institute for the Gifted. I submitted a cover letter and résumé. A few weeks later, I got a call. I was hired to teach the Art of Improvisation. SIG rented classroom space at Sarah Lawrence College in Bronxville. My class would meet Monday–Thursday at 1:00–2:30 p.m. My students were in middle school. A few weeks after being hired to teach the improvisation class, I got another call from SIG. I was asked if I'd be interested in teaching an additional class that met in the morning.

"Sure," I said. "What's the course?"

"The Art of Hieroglyphics."

"Interesting. What's the age group?"

"Five-year-olds."

Who was I to be offered a position like this? The closest level I'd come to teaching this age group was middle school. I'd never taken any early childhood education classes. Maybe it was more important that the job be filled as opposed to filling it with the right person? It was a good thing I had an affectionate fascination for young children.

The children were magnificent. I'd break out into a sloppy grin the minute they walked into the class. They came from upper-middle to upper-class homes. I had about sixteen students. Two children shared a desk. They were all given plenty of drawing paper and different colored magic markers. The course's main objective was to teach them how to create their own system of symbols to which they were to assign the different sounds that comprised the English language. Maybe the staff at SIG thought I could teach this because it was linked to phonetics? Even so, there I was, trying to teach young children how to construct a sound system while some of them were just learning how to read! It wasn't easy. But how hard could it be to float around from desk to desk and look into the eyes of expectant, innocent, beautifully behaved children? And I had a teaching assistant as well.

My Art of Improvisation class was a bit of a headache. The students were just returning from lunch. When they were focused on theatre games, they were fine and often interesting to watch. But when they became restless and unfocused, my assistant and I joined forces and became more like commandants. All in all, the summer of 2017 at SIG was a rewarding and enriching experience, and both the tykes and pubescents liked me. And the money was fair. Too bad the weekly commute to Bronxville was seventy-six clams.

On the last day of class of SIG's three-week session, as my Art of Hieroglyphics class filed out, young Olivia handed me a piece of paper. It was eight-by-eleven letter-sized paper that was longitudinally folded. On the cover, drawn in brown magic marker, was a circle resembling a sun. Underneath Olivia's sun, she printed my name. Underneath my name, she drew a window. Underneath the window, she drew a cone. Olivia filled the cone with crisscrossed lines, attempting to suggest a house.

When I opened the page, I read:

Thank you for
Teaching
Me letters
+ numbers
So I made you
A card to make
You feel the
Same way.

> I hope you enjoy it
> See ya next year! xo xo
> Olivia

And at the upper top right of the page's crease, Olivia wrote, "You're sweet." And a few inches down, she taped a small packet of Striking Popping Candy, green apple flavor.

In the middle of August, I found a post from Indeed seeking an adjunct for the Speech and Theater Department at Borough of Manhattan Community College. I sent a cover letter and résumé. I received an e-mail from a Dr. Jones. I went over for an interview. He was a wiry thirty-something. The interview lasted all of three minutes. What was to decide? I already had experience at BMCC.

Before I left the room, Dr. Jones said "Yes, I'm going to be using you."

This was about a week and a half before the semester started, just like I'd previously been hired at BMCC. Days passed with no word from Dr. Jones. The Sunday before the semester began, I took a chance and called Dr. Jones in his office. He answered.

"Just wondering when you'll know the appointments for the fall," I inquired.

"You know you're not making this any easier," Dr. Jones replied. "I'm still deciding."

The next morning, Dr. Jones e-mailed my schedule. He assigned me two Fundamentals of Speech courses. Both began at eight in the morning. One of them met once a week on Sundays for three hours.

At Mercy, my days at Dobbs Ferry came to an end because a full-time professor returned to the department after trying a senior administration position. Now I'd be teaching at Mercy's Manhattan site on West Thirty-Fourth Street, just off Sixth Avenue. And my load was increased to three courses. Not bad. But how I missed looking through the window on Metro North at the sun-dappled Hudson River during the quiet of a Friday afternoon.

On spring of 2018, my schedule was the same but for one less course at BMCC. My course met once a week on Monday afternoons in Washington Heights at a site dubbed CUNY in the Heights. It was a small section and quite a mixed bag of students. A student from West Africa was the most serious and disciplined of all. There was a young man from Phoenix, Arizona, who informed me very early on that he sometimes forgot to "take his meds."

"For what condition are you taking medication, if I may ask?"

"It's hard to explain."

I was observed one afternoon by Dr. Jones.

He informed me beforehand that he would arrive when class began and leave after about an hour or when I took a break. When I informed the class that everyone could now take a short break, Dr. Jones just up and left without even looking at me. When I met him in his office for our post-observation discussion, I couldn't get over the cross he wore over such a finely pressed white shirt and azure tie. He gave me an overall favorable evaluation. But then Dr. Jones mentioned that adjunct reappointments were always dependent on adequate courses running and "sufficient" student enrollment.

"I've known that since you were bouncing on your grandpappy's knee," I felt like saying.

A few weeks later, I received BMCC's official notice informing me that I would not be reappointed for the fall.

In May of 2018, I staged the full-length *Children Are Forever; All Sales Are Final* for the Strawberry Play Festival at Shelter Studios in Manhattan. The play explores the bureaucratic red tape a Los Angeles interracial lesbian couple experiences while trying to legally adopt a child from an agency in Atlanta, Georgia. A few weeks before the play opened, I went to the Speech and Theater Department at BMCC to check my mail box in the adjunct office. There I met another adjunct, a young woman. We got to talking, and then the subject of conversation fell on the play I was currently directing. The young woman seemed to take quite an interest in this. Then she asked me if I were at all interested in teaching Oral Communications at Bergen Community College. She taught there and found out from the chair that there would be opportunities.

"Sure," I said.

"Send me you résumé, and then I'll forward it to Dr. Johnson."
I sent her my résumé that very day.

A few days later, I received an e-mail from a Kendra, the founder and director of Laurissa Jane Arts Camp in Laurelton, Queens. I'd answered an ad she posted on Craigslist. She had an opening for a director of the camp's summer musical, *Mulan Jr.* Kendra and I met at a coffee shop on the Bowery. She brought the book and score with her. I was hired on the spot.

Mulan Jr. is based on Disney's animated *Mulan*, which is based on a Chinese legend. It's the story of teenaged Hua Mulan, who, after failing her betrothal ceremony, ultimately disguises herself as a boy in order to help defend the Chinese Empire from the ruthless attack of Shan-Yu and his Huns. It's an action-adventure musical with multiple settings and many parts large and small. I'd be paid twenty dollars per hour, working from 9:45 to 11:45 a.m. on Monday–Thursday. I'd begin the last week of June, and the show opened for two performances the first week of August. The commute wasn't easy. I took the E train to the last stop in Jamaica, then changed for a bus. From door to door, it took an hour and fifteen minutes.

At Laurissa Jane Arts camp with my wonderful cast of
Disney's *Mulan Jr.* A mic's just as good as a bullhorn!

The camp was held in a public school in Laurelton's residential section, with its modest colonials and mostly manicured lawns. When I got off the bus, it was only a block to the school's entrance. I walked up a few steps, greeted a portly security guard, turned left, and walked through the cafeteria. Then I reached a hallway and classrooms that served as the base for the camp.

On my very first day, as I approached the main classroom, I heard the music of Erik Satie. When I opened the door, there was Kendra, her assistant, a counselor, and the campers. The campers ranged in age from five to fourteen. They were seated at desks, quietly engaged in craft work to Erik Satie's Gymnopedie. Kendra lowered the music and asked for the campers' attention. She gave me a warm introduction. Some of the kids greeted me with a hello. Others nodded. Some smiled.

In a few minutes, we were off to the auditorium for auditions. We gave all the campers a chance to read some lines from the script and sing a few bars from the score. We gave the role of Mulan to one of the older females. We assigned the other roles as if we were assigning field positions to a Little League baseball squad. I didn't feel qualified for this job. A peppy undergraduate theatre student could have filled the position quite adequately. Yet I sensed I was brought on to establish order and project authority.

To begin rehearsals, I was handed a microphone that was linked to an amplifier. The kids lacked discipline, had trouble remembering the simplest of my given stage directions, couldn't act, and could sing a little. They were better in chorus than in solos. And they were wonderful and a joy to work with. They were respectful and unspoiled, happy to be where they were. I never heard a crossword pass between them. And there was no foul language. I believe Miss Kendra saw to that. A positive vibe filled the air. I'd stage the scenes in the morning, and in the afternoon, the kids worked on the musical numbers with a young choreographer, a pleasant lad in his late twenties. After the third week of rehearsals, the choreographer joined in on the morning rehearsals.

By then, I seemed like an unnecessary appendage. I'd staged the scenes and given the kids some rudimentary insight into the characters they were playing and the dramatic circumstances. Now it was just a matter of keeping the traffic fluid, making sure they spoke their lines loud enough to be heard, and reminding them where they needed to be for their entrances and exits. When I arrived in the morning, I'd occasionally work some of the scenes with dialogue that included two to three characters. Then everyone would go to the auditorium. I'd sit in the middle of the house as more or less a silent supervisor to the entire production.

If the kids weren't concentrating at all, I'd walk up to the stage, stop the proceedings, and say, "What's wrong with everyone today? You were so much better yesterday. Come back."

Sometimes I'd take a little one aside to strengthen a line delivery. The littlest ones were cast as Hun soldiers or Chinese soldiers. I'd take them by the hand and lead them to the hallway.

If the child had a line like "Captain! We must forge on ahead! Glory to the Chinese Empire!" I'd simply say, "Good. Now watch and listen." Then I gave an overly theatrical and artificially gestural delivery. Then I'd say, "Now you do it the way I did it." And they'd come through. Then I said "Bravo. Good, good, very good. Maybe you can do it like that all the time?" I got results with this method.

At the conclusion of the first performance, Kendra asked all the campers to wait on stage. Then she said a few words to the audience about the summer's success and how all the parents should be proud. Then she asked the campers to take a few steps back to allow the staff members to come on stage and take a bow to the audience's applause. After the staff had been introduced, it was time to take pictures. I asked Kendra if I could pose with all the campers and fellow staff.

That night, I wore a black polo shirt and black shorts. The campers and staff were lined up in four rows. The younger ones in the first two rows, the elder and taller ones in the third row, Kendra and counselors standing on a platform in the fourth row. I staged the photo thus: I'm sitting in a chair, downstage left at the end of the first row. I took off my sandals and I crossed my legs. I chose two of the youngest campers to stand on either side of me—one male the other female. When looking at the color printout, the viewer's eye can't help but finally arrive at my lily-white crossed legs protruding from my black shorts. They look like a pair of raw drumsticks, freshly severed and haphazardly discarded to a butcher's block, configured to a forty-five-degree angle.

The summer of 2018 also marked my return to the Secret Theatre's Short Play Festival in Long Island City where, the previous January, I directed a drama about AIDS research. This time, it was a delightful comedy about Mary Roget inspiring her physician husband to work through his linguistic obsessions to create what we now know as *Roget's Thesaurus*.

Keeping with CUNY's tradition of hiring adjuncts at the eleventh hour, Bronx Community College contacted me a week before fall semester 2018 began. I'd answered a classified on Indeed posted by the Communication Arts and Science Department. I took the number 2 train to Grand Concourse in the South Bronx at 149th Street and Third Avenue. Then I walked upstairs and connected to a number 4 or 5 to Burnside Avenue. I descended the stairs to El Barrio in all its shameless vitality. I turned left and made my way up a steep and winding Burnside Avenue. I came to Dr. Martin Luther King Boulevard and made a right. It was as steep as Burnside Avenue. In about three minutes, I arrived at the enclosed campus of Bronx Community College.

I walked under the arch and up five flights of seven-stepped stairs. On my left was a string of bedraggled administrative buildings save for a converted house that served as Human Resources. On my right, there's a dirt running track surrounding a dual baseball diamond and football field complete with goal posts. Past the field was a quad consisting of North Hall and Library, Hall of Philosophy, Library of New York University, and Hall of Languages. Each structure resembled the Nereid Monument, but they were all baseless whose columns were a random mix of Ionic, Doric, and Corinthian. Past the quad was the Hall of Fame, a serpentine path that featured no less than ninety-six mounted bronze busts of famous authors, educators, scientists, soldiers, jurists, and statesman. There were many a sunny morn when I'd saunter over to the Hall of Fame and have imaginary conversations with the likes of Emerson, Poe, Teddy Roosevelt, and Walt Whitman.

Bronx Community College was certainly a campus in search of a cogent identity. Nevertheless, it was by far the most interesting one I'd ever set foot on. More's the pity that I only lasted one semester. I was offered one course for spring, but it conflicted with my Saturday Mercy course. When I contacted the chair to keep me in mind for other courses should they become available, she didn't acknowledge my e-mail.

Sometime in late October, I was contacted by Dr. Johnson over at Bergen Community College. She suddenly had an opening for a couple of communication courses and asked if I could take over. "Thanks so much for thinking of me, but I'm committed at those times," I said in a reply e-mail. We arranged for a face-to-face interview to explore future opportunities.

Dr. Johnson conveyed a warm tone in her e-mails and matched it when I met her in her office. We briefly talked about my teaching approach, and she asked me if I would be interested in teaching film courses. At the interview's conclusion, Dr. Johnson gave me a packet of forms to fill out for Human Resources. I also had to submit three letters of recommendation from sources familiar with my college teaching. It looked like I'd now be venturing to the frontiers of the Garden State.

By mid-November, Dr. Johnson had offered me three courses—one Oral Communications and two Interpersonal Communications. The Interpersonal Communications courses met on Tuesday and Thursday mornings from 8:00 to 9:15 a.m. and then from 9:30 to 10:45 a.m. I awakened around 5:30 a.m. I took a 163 New Jersey Transit bus out of Port Authority. The latest bus I could take was a 6:30. I usually took the 6:20 a.m.

My Oral Communications class met once a week on Thursday afternoon, from 1:45 to 4:30. This presented a bit of a problem. My usual late Saturday morning class at Mercy was cancelled due to inadequate enrollment. This had never happened to me before at Mercy. But given Mercy's loyalty and appreciation for my past work, I was given an early Thursday evening section of Understanding Movies.

This class met at 6:10 p.m. I could never be on time for Understanding Movies due to my Thursday afternoon class at Bergen. The bus ride back to Port Authority from Bergen Community College could be up to an hour and forty minutes in late afternoon traffic. The first bus leaving Bergen after my Oral Communications class left at 4:45 p.m. That meant I'd arrive no earlier than 6:40 p.m. to my Understanding Movies class. No problem at all.

I ended my Oral Communications class at Bergen at 4:00 p.m. I would teach class without a break. Then I'd make a 4:20 p.m. bus and arrive in Port Authority around 6:00. It could be a twenty-minute walk from Port Authority at 42nd Street and Eighth Avenue to Mercy College at 34th Street and Sixth Avenue. The sidewalks teem with the rush-hour mob. When I arrived at Port Authority, I hastened to the street and made my way through the mob as quickly as I could without bumping into anyone. I'd made an agreement with my Mercy students that class would promptly begin no later than 6:30 p.m. and that we'd go without a break to 8:40, the official time class ended.

After teaching a two-hour and fifteen-minute class, riding a bus for an hour and forty minutes, and making my way on foot for twenty minutes at the peak of Manhattan's rush hour, I arrived at Mercy in quite the state. I was short of breath, a bit lightheaded, and ever so happy to be teaching a subject I loved!

My first semester teaching at Bergen Community College went well enough. You could engage the students in open discussion. Not a few of them were very well spoken. And it was nice to get out of the city to a suburban campus. I liked the ride. When the bus emerged in the early morning from the Lincoln Tunnel, it passed the Hudson River, granting me a brief view of Manhattan's downtown skyline. Against the Aegean blue sky, it resembled one of those twinkling backdrops that loom behind a late-night talk show host. At the front end of the bus, there was a rectangular panel stating the upcoming stops in red-neon text.

Accompanying the panel's listings was a prerecorded announcement. The first stop in Weehawken was Marginal and Pleasant. At 6:10 in the morning, I was not quite pleasant, but I could certainly feel on the margins of the mainstream workforce. Among the mostly working-class Hispanic passengers, I could well imagine myself a migrant worker riding in a school bus in predawn California on my way to Central Valley for a sun-to-sun shift to pick apricots and be paid by the bushel. The dream lasted for as long as I let it before I returned to reality as the bus progressed through northeastern New Jersey. We passed through Union City, East Rutherford, Hasbrouck Heights, Maywood, and Rochelle Park. I liked the many mom-and-pop businesses I saw along the way, from bakeshops to flower shops to a pet-grooming salon to launderettes.

We finally arrived at Bergen Community College in Paramus. As soon as I arrived, about eighty feet due north, I saw a green octagonal sign posted atop a mound of gray soil. In hand-painted white letters, it read, "Orchard Hills," and below this "Bergen County Golf Course." To the left was the first tee. There were some sunny early spring mornings when I'd see someone preparing to tee off. If his attention suddenly veered in my direction, I'd smile and wave. Not a bad way to start a day's work.

For winter/spring 2019, I was back on the boards, directing two one-acts plays at Manhattan Repertory in midtown Manhattan— *You Just Don't Understand* and *Wyatt Earp's Jewish Adventure*. The former detailed a marriage's deterioration, and the latter, the courtship of Jewess Josephine Marcus and gentile lawman Wyatt Earp. In *You Just Don't Understand*, I played the husband of said troubled marriage, and in *Wyatt Earp's Jewish Adventure*, I played Josephine's father, Hyman. It was the first time any character addressed me as "papa" on stage. During the summer of 2019, I directed *The Secret File of J. Edgar Hoover* at Manhattan Rep and *Beardy McBearderson* at the Secret Theatre's Short Play Festival.

For my work at Manhattan Rep, the playwright paid me a mere pittance, but I was paid $500 to direct *Beardy McBearderson*, which explored the zany behavior of a hardcore vlogger. Toward the end of the summer, I directed a play about a young Turk in Los Angeles faced with sudden deportation called *Not That Illegal* at Strawberry One-Act Festival. Coupled with my theatre work was my usual

Monday evening summer course at Mercy's Manhattan site. It was a wonderful summer.

In mid-July came the most prestigious opportunity of my modest directing career. I answered a post on Playbill.com seeking a director for a new full-length to be staged at the famed Players Theatre on McDougal Street in Greenwich Village. After submitting my résumé, a cover letter, and a recommendation, I got a response from the playwright/co-producer. We arranged an interview. *Thank You for Taking My Call* would be performed for a three-week, twelve-performance Actors' Equity—approved showcase.

Opening night was slated for Thursday, September 12th. My interview was held in a tiny, hourly rented room in an office building in the west forties. Gill and I talked for about ten minutes. He asked me about my approach to rehearsals. About a week later, I received an e-mail from Gill. The subject line read, "You're the man!" When I spoke with Gill on the phone, he explained to me that out of the twenty or so directors he interviewed, he enjoyed my answers the most. I was paid $500.00, too little for the work involved, but I happily overlooked it, given the project's caliber.

Thank You for Taking My Call was promoted through several media outlets, had a twelve-performance run, hired professionals for lighting and sound design, and used three Equity actors out of a cast of four. Our non-Equity actor could very well have been Equity what with his blazing talent and discipline. And he played the leading role, an angry and confrontational radio talk show host.

The performances had good houses. I got along swimmingly with the cast and earned their respect. These were pros with experience and solid credits. Up until that point, I'd mostly worked with amateurs or kids trying to break into the business. Some were fine and talented. But you often need to remind them what transpired during the last rehearsal, and you'd often see little evidence of homework or genuine character growth. Not so with the cast of *Thank You for Taking My Call.* It reminded me of the difference between teaching graduate students their major field of study and witnessing growth as opposed to teaching a required course to undergraduates.

I was reappointed to Bergen for fall of 2019. This time, I was assigned two sections of Oral Communications. Classes met on Mondays and Wednesdays. I had the same 8:00 a.m. class as before and, after that, a 12:20 p.m.–1:35 p.m. class. I liked the downtime because much of it was used for the writing of this memoir. I was assigned my usual three courses at Mercy. This time, my Saturday morning class ran. There was a Friday morning class and a Monday/Wednesday evening class from 5:50 to 8:20 p.m. that met for seven weeks. This turned out to be one of my toughest gigs ever.

I'd teach my second class at Bergen on Mondays and Wednesday until 1:35 p.m. Then I had an hour and a half bus ride back to Manhattan. I arrived at Mercy close to 4:00 p.m. with another two hours of downtime until my next class at 5:50 p.m. By the time I'd arrive at Mercy, my energy was spent. I started my day at 5:30 in the morning. By the end of my 5:50 Mercy class, I'd put in close to a fifteen-hour day with almost six hours of teaching.

I was no longer a boy, but I went the distance and put out for those Monday/Wednesday evening classes. There were nights when I even channeled more energy than called for as a way of rousing myself to the occasion. Yet this was a much easier gig to adjust to than my twice weekly commute to Bergen, which finally began bearing its fangs. As with so many other new experiences I had as an adjunct, when the novelty wore thin, stubborn reality set in. And this happened when fall of 2019 began.

While riding the New Jersey Transit bus on my way to Bergen, I slowly but surely became aware of just how many times the bus stopped. With red lights, stop signs, picking up of passengers, and dropping off of passengers, the bus made no less than fifty stops during an hour's ride. It wasn't so much the red lights and stop signs that bothered me. It was the dropping off and picking up of passengers. It was not unusual for the bus to drop off a passenger, travel forty feet, and pick up or drop off another passenger.

There were times when a passenger pushed the stop request button to be let out. Some forty feet, and twenty seconds later, another passenger would do the same. Like an octogenarian in corrective sneakers leading the pack in a cross-country race over mountainous terrain, there was something perversely incongruent to a hulky motor coach bus incessantly stopping along small-town main streets and suburban roads. I called New Jersey Transit to inquire about alternative routes back to Manhattan. I was told that the 175 bus to Manhattan was a shorter ride with less stops than the 163, and that its last stop was the George Washington Bridge Terminal.

From there, I could walk downstairs and catch a D train to Thirty-Fifth Street to teach at Mercy or catch an A train home. I tried taking the 175. It reached Manhattan in a shorter time, and I liked crossing the George Washington Bridge. But there were still too many stops in between ridiculously short distances. Sometimes the tires screeched when the bus came to a slow stop, calling to mind a school of virginal whales in heat.

One time, I boarded the wrong 175 bus. The bus I needed to take me across the GWB was the 175, Garden State. I got on the 175, Ridgewood. This occurred on the last evening of my Monday/Wednesday class at Mercy. I was to administer my final exam. I realized about twenty minutes into the ride that I was passing unfamiliar streets and neighborhoods. It was getting late, and I was getting nervous. I went up to the driver and asked him if he went to the George Washington Bridge.

"Yeah, man! I go to de bridge!"

I returned to my seat. A young woman asked me where I wanted to go.

"Across the GWB to the terminal."

Then she told me that this bus stopped *near* the bridge but didn't cross it. For that, I needed the 175, Garden State. Panic set in. It was now going on 5:00 p.m. My Mercy class would start in fifty minutes, and I was nowhere near the bridge. I went over to the bus driver and asked him how much longer before we reached the bridge, and he crossly said in his Caribbean Island accent, "Soon, man! I tell you, man, we get to de bridge soon!"

"Soon" turned out to be another twenty-five minutes.

As soon as I saw the bridge, I asked the young woman when I should get off the bus.

I got off somewhere in Fort Lee. It was now 5:30 p.m. I didn't have an iPhone, so I couldn't e-mail my students through Mercy College's website. I had a cell phone, but I didn't have any of the students' phone numbers to call one of them to inform them that I would be late. But even if I did, it wouldn't matter because my cell phone had run out of juice. I couldn't even call Mercy's security desk. It was an unseasonably warm late October afternoon. I was wearing sandals over socks. The skin in between my left foot's toes became irritated. Through some miracle, I made my way to the toll booths at the bridge's entrance. I approached a toll booth.

The clerk said, "Hey, brothah!"

"I wanna walk across the bridge."

He graciously gave me directions. I turned and continued my trek. I was completely lost. I stopped at the driver's side to an idle rig sitting at the edge of a small construction site and asked the driver where the entrance to the bridge path was. He pointed his iPhone over my head and mumbled some directions. In a few minutes (which seemed a merciless eternity), I reach the bridge's pathway. It was now after 6:00 p.m. It was a mile's walk over the bridge. Thank goodness it was still light out. I couldn't even name the river I was walking over. Bicyclists passed me, as did some people who looked to be walking home after a day's work. I walked the mile across the bridge in record time, but it was the longest mile I had ever walked.

I reached the George Washington Bridge terminal by 6:25 p.m. I got on a D train. It was packed. A crazed and drunken panhandler entered the subway car while singing a grossly off-key version of Bill Wither's gold single "Lean on Me." I dropped a quarter in his cup.

I finally made it to class by 6:45 p.m., almost an hour late. As soon as I walked through the door, a female student asked, "Are you all right?"

"I'm fine. Thank you for asking."

During the opening scene of the musical *Fiddler on the Roof*, dairyman Tevye is reflecting on the community of Anatevka. He asks the audience, "Why do we stay here?" Then he continues, "Well, Anatevka is our home."

You might well ask me, "Why have you continued to be an adjunct? Can't a man with your abilities find a more stable and secure—not to mention better paying—position?"

I suppose so. But, well, I continue to do this because this is what I do. And the rewards outweigh the costs. I've always had trouble with authority. As an adjunct instructor, there's no one watching over my shoulder and checking out my work. I can handle the occasional observation, but other than that, I have about as much autonomy as one could ask for. I have material to cover, but the words I use and the method to my approach is no one's business but my own. A text-book is merely a blueprint to my own creative lesson plan.

I'm too restless to sit behind a desk for eight hours, and I truly believe that all this running around for the past thirty years has been good for my health. I'm now pushing sixty but look and feel younger. I'm what you'd call a true independent, ever ready to embrace new challenges alone and weather sudden setbacks with grace and for-titude. I'm like Melville's "migratory foul that in flight never heeds when it crosses a frontier." Perhaps I suggest a likeness to Burns's field mouse, a "wee, sleekit, cowerin', timorous beastie." Maybe I'm somewhere between? Maybe I'm a whiskered and bespectacled fish-bird running on a suspended treadmill over prickly embers in a cage with door ajar to let plenty of sunshine in? I like to think of myself as a species that defies category. And I like my work. And I've even carved out a modest but consistent career directing in the theatre. I'm paid for my work and it brings out the best in me and channels my humanity. This is important because sometimes an Adjunct might work for rude and unkind people, people who would corrode one's humanity. If you cannot find joy in the work, God pity you.

I'm currently doing dramaturgical work for two playwrights. This past October, I directed a staged reading of a new musical, *My Father's Play*. Since then, the composer/producer has made several revisions and also plans another upscale staged reading with yours truly at the helm for an invited audience of potential backers for a full-scale Off-Broadway production. I'm currently teaching my usual three courses at Mercy but in a new and very much improved location. Mercy moved its Manhattan address in fall 2019 from Thirty-Fifth Street and Sixth to Thirty-Fourth Street. We now occupy the third and fourth floors and will have more floors and student housing to come. The third floor consists of a huge student lounge complete with tables, sofas, settees, plastic-enclosed cubicles with widescreen desktops, and a small cafeteria. It's a state-of-the-art college facility that offers a panoramic view of Herald Square through soundproof, ceiling-high windows.

I have an airy and high-ceilinged office that I share with other adjuncts, but I will often have the office to myself, and I have storage space for my books and files. Adjuncts at Mercy have finally unionized, and we have recently received a 30 percent increase in wages for a three-credit course. I can walk to Mercy from my apartment in twenty minutes. This offsets the maddening commute to Bergen, where I've been reappointed. I'm currently teaching Oral Communications and Introduction to Cinema.

I still cringe at all those bus stops. If I could afford to commission a chemist to design a temporary sedative to inure me to them, I would. But I will simply cope. I must. Who has a choice not to in the world of labor?

I don't plan on retiring. I have more ambition and see more possibilities in theatre than I do in academia. Remember that I'm a lifer, and lifers serve out their sentences to the very end of the line. It's been a long and strange and sometimes literally bumpy trip. It's not over. At least I've enjoyed the ride.

New York City, 2020

About the Author

Laurence C. Schwartz began teaching at university in 1989. He has taught at twenty different universities and twenty-three different subjects, including Introduction to Opera, Introduction to Theater, Business Communication, The Hollywood Western, Art History, Cinema Studies, History of American Music, and Public Speaking.

In addition to his university lectures, Schwartz is a theater director, actor, and writer. He is the author of the full-length play Artaud for Awhile, in which he portrayed the French poet Antonin Artaud at Wings Theatre in Greenwich Village, New York City. In 2019, Schwartz directed Thank You for Taking My Call at the Players Theatre. In 2018, he directed A Family Christmas Reunion at the Davenport Theatre. Schwartz has directed over a dozen plays in New York for Riant Theatre's Strawberry One-Act Festival. He has also directed at Manhattan Rep and the Secret Theatre.

For several years, he was director-in-residence at the American Theatre of Actors. Schwartz has had several one-act plays produced in New York. His short fiction has been published in The Pink Chameleon, StarryNight Review, The Paumanok Review, In Posse Review, and American Feed. He received his BFA from Boston University and his MA from Hunter College—CUNY.

He currently teaches speech communications and film at Mercy College. He lives in Manhattan with attorney Vanessa Ramcharan and their two felines.

CPSIA information can be obtained
at www.ICGtesting.com
Printed in the USA
BVHW021643080322
630895BV00020B/1003